THE MIRACLES OF JESUS

JOSEPH RHYMER

THE MIRACLES OF JESUS

SP St Paul Publications

Cover design by Diane Edward

St Paul Publications
Middlegreen, Slough SL3 6BT, United Kingdom

© Joseph Rhymer 1991

ISBN 085439 387 0

Printed by Ashford Colour Press, Gosport

St Paul Publications is an activity of the priests and brothers of the Society of St Paul who proclaim the Gospel through the media of social communication

Contents

Preface   7

1. Questions and answers about miracles   9

2. Gospels and miracles   15

3. Nature miracles   29

4. Resurrection miracles   49

5. Healing blind people   59

6. Miracles of healing various faculties   69

7. Other miracles of healing   83

8. Exorcisms of demons   95

9. The four gospels and their miracles   109

10. The miracles and the significance of Jesus   135

Index of miracles in the four gospels   141

The miracles and the Liturgy   147

Suggestions for further reading   151

Preface

The miracles of Jesus are only one part of a much wider picture, the whole pattern of early Christian beliefs about Jesus. If this fact is ignored the gospel records of the miracles can be dismissed as descriptions of mere acts of magic, or gross exaggerations by Christian propagandists who had a vested interest in inflating the importance of their founder. Without this wider picture the miracles of Jesus may also be dismissed as naive explanations by people living in a pre-scientific age who believed that the gods controlled even the ordinary events of everyday life.

This study of the miracles aims to show how the first Christians selected and arranged their information about Jesus to illustrate and support their beliefs. The miracles were just part of the evidence presented by those who had known Jesus, to help their followers to realize who Jesus really was, what he had achieved for them, and how he continued to affect their lives.

Aims such as these imply that the miracles of Jesus only make full sense to believing Christians; this is deliberate, for the same assumption is also implied in everything the four gospels record. The wider picture to which the miracles belong consists of the broad sweep of beliefs about Jesus held by the first Christians, which determined the way the gospels were written.

These were not blind beliefs which people accepted merely because they were preached by the disciples of Jesus who had known him personally. The first Christians tested and confirmed what they were taught about Jesus, and they were assured of its truth by the effect it had on their everyday lives. We can see that process of verification at work in the frank and detailed letters they wrote to each other during the sixty years or so immediately following the death and resurrection of Jesus, letters which have been preserved in the New Testament along with the four gospels.

This book begins with a brief examination of the kind of questions we can ask about the miracles, and how the questions affect the answers we give. It then examines the way in which the miracles contribute to the general picture of Jesus presented in the gospels. Each of the miracles is then examined in more detail, with a separate chapter given to each kind: nature miracles, resurrection miracles, various kinds of healing miracles, and exorcisms.

The first of the two concluding chapters examines the way each of the gospels fits the miracles into its structure to support its particular aims. The final chapter draws the threads together to show how the miracles helped the first Christians to apply their beliefs about Jesus to their everyday lives.

We all live by a pattern of beliefs even if we are not fully aware of what those beliefs really are. Whatever our beliefs about Jesus may be, a study of the accounts of the miracles will help us to find what we actually believe, so that we can given an honest answer to the question put by Jesus to the Pharisees: 'What do you think of the Christ? Whose son is he?' (Mt 22:42).

1

Questions and answers about miracles

Next only to the crucifixion and resurrection, the miracles of Jesus are the most dramatic of all the events reported in the gospels and the most controversial. Many just dismiss them as fiction; others think they are exaggerated versions of more mundane events; some take them literally. For some people they are the strongest evidence for their Christian beliefs, but the same stories cause others the strongest doubts. Much of this confusion about the miracles of Jesus is caused by the kind of questions people ask about them.

Several different kinds of questions can be asked: What actually happened? Why did Jesus do them? What effect did they have on the people who were present? Why did the first Christians record them in the four gospels? These questions yield very different kinds of answers, as we can see if we ask the same kind of questions about a modern surgeon and the operations he or she performs on the patients brought for treatment.

With such modern technology as cameras, video-tapes and films, it would be easy to make a complete factual record of a surgical operation as it was being done, in order to see what actually happens when a surgeon operates. Such a record would then be available to future generations for reference and analysis. If we want to know what actually happened when Jesus performed his miracles, we have to turn to the gospel records based on the reports of people who were present.

There might seem to be a problem here because these reports first circulated by word of mouth and were only recorded in writing many years later. However, we need not be too worried by this. Oral tradition can be very accurate when it is the responsibility of a stable community of people. The accuracy of the information quickly becomes a group responsibility, especially when the original witnesses are still present. The first Christian Churches at the beginning of the New Testament period were just such stable communities, and the twelve apostles were still there to authenticate the stories about Jesus.

The problem of what actually happened when Jesus performed the miracles arises because we only have the records provided by the four gospels, with no independent confirmation from other sources. This makes it important for us to face the fact that the four gospels are faith documents, not independent, objective records. They were written to support a particular set of beliefs about Jesus, and these beliefs permeate every page of them. A reader of the gospels who does not accept these underlying beliefs will be unlikely to accept the stories of the miracles as reliable accounts of what actually happened. On the other hand, reading the accounts of the miracles may move someone to accept the beliefs and make the act of faith, even though the question of what actually happened cannot be answered objectively.

The next kind of question is, 'Why does a surgeon perform operations on people?' There can only be one satisfactory answer to that. A surgeon performs an operation on a person in need of medical help simply because the surgeon has the skill to deal with the sickness and the sick person is brought to the surgeon for treatment.

This is exactly the kind of answer we must give if we ask why Jesus performed miracles. Jesus did them when he was faced with a situation which required his special powers and skills. He would meet a leper as he travelled along a road; a crowd would come to hear him teach and he found that they had no food with them; a mother would tell him about her daughter, lying ill at home, or a soldier about his servant; he would notice a disabled man while teaching in a synagogue on a Sabbath and he would heal him; a blind man would call out as he passed.

The encounters were accidental, or they occurred because people had heard about Jesus' reputation as a healer and they sought him out. Jesus would usually act immediately to meet the sick person's need. The miracles were not performed by Jesus in order to back up his personal claims as Messiah, even if this is why his disciples later told people about them. Like the surgeon, he acted out of compassion for the person in need, not to prove what powers he had. Jesus main purposes during his ministry were to teach whoever would listen to him, to train his disciples and, above all as Messiah to bear witness to God.

The miracles did, however, produce effects far beyond Jesus immediate intention, so we can ask, 'What effect did they have on the people who were present?' Some people were angered by them. Narrowly legalistic religious authorities saw them as breaches of the divine law if Jesus healed people on the Sabbath. Some of the authorities saw them as threats to their own power, and they told people that Jesus undoubted powers were evil ones. He could defeat evil, they said, because he was more evil than any of the evil which tried to defy him.

When his disciples saw Jesus perform miracles it contributed powerfully to the attitudes they must develop if they were to continue Jesus work. Medical students learn as they watch an expert surgeon operating; the surgeon does not operate primarily to teach the students or to demonstrate his powers, but these are secondary results of what he does. So too with Jesus' miracles. When the disciples saw Jesus heal or exorcise, they appreciated more fully who Jesus really was and how he went about his work.

Finally, we can ask why the gospels recorded the miracles of Jesus. As we shall see, the gospels contain records of thirty-six miracles, but these are only a fraction of the miracles Jesus is reputed to have done. The number of miracles each gospel records ranges from just eight in John's Gospel to more than twenty in Luke's. No one gospel records all the miracles recorded in any other gospel, and no gospel arranges them in the same order as any other one. Clearly, the gospels do not record the miracles merely because they happened. They have some other purpose in mind.

We shall be looking at this purpose more closely, but at this stage it is sufficient to say that all four gospels have one fundamental aim. They provide their readers, the first Christians, with support material for the message about Jesus – the 'good news' – which they had heard from his apostles. That message centred on the crucifixion and resurrection, and what God had done for his world through Jesus in those three decisive days. In short, although Jesus had suffered death he had also risen from the dead, and all who repented of their sins and believed in him as saviour could share in his eternal life.

Each gospel concentrates on that act of redemption and devotes a full third of its space to it. Each gospel also selects events from the earlier part of Jesus' life to help readers to understand the full significance of his death and resurrection. The gospels' miracle stories are part of that support material, selected to enrich the faith of their particular readers. The four gospels differ in the way they do this only because they were first written for four different groups of Christians from different backgrounds.

The biography of a surgeon only records a selection of the operations he or she performed. The selection is made to illustrate the full range of the surgeon's abilities, and perhaps the selection is arranged so that they all focus on some outstanding feature of his or her character or some climax in his or her life which gives the reader an insight into everything that happened. The gospels are not biographies of Jesus, they are faith documents, but like biographies they focus on an outstanding feature of Jesus which explain everything he did – that he is the messianic Son of God incarnate, come to redeem.

The miracles are not the only material selected by the gospel writers to bring out the full significance of Jesus.

There are also parables, sermons, friendships and rejections, discussions and confrontations, and a wide range of encounters with many different kinds of people. Even the stories of Jesus' birth and infancy were recorded with all the advantage of hindsight, so they also are told in a way which points forward to the crucifixion and resurrection.

Much of the information and comment in the rest of this book will appear to separate the miracles from this other gospel material about Jesus. It is necessary to do this in order to highlight the special contribution made by the miracles to the gospel story, but their full significance can only be appreciated by putting them back in their place again along with the other material selected by the gospels. Even then, their significance will be lost if they are not viewed from the vantage point of the faith and the beliefs they originally supported.

2

Gospels and miracles

'That evening, at sundown, they brought to him all who were sick or possessed with demons. And the whole city was gathered together about the door. And he healed many who were sick with various diseases, and cast out many demons; and he would not permit the demons to speak, because they knew him'

(Mk 1:32-34).

Then Jesus, aged about 30, started his public ministry in the part of Palestine where he had spent his childhood, he rapidly acquired a reputation as a miracle-worker. That reputation grew and spread wherever he went. Quite apart from his many acts of healing, he also did things which clash with normal natural laws, such as walking on water, calming a storm and using very little food to feed large crowds. He raised dead people to life again and overcame a wide variety of evil forces. According to the four gospels, he continued to do such things throughout his ministry until finally he himself rose again from death after his public execution, and ascended into the clouds in front of a crowd of witnesses.

Because the miracles are such vividly memorable incidents it is easy to think about them in isolation, without considering how they fit into the rest of the material about Jesus and the general pattern of the gospels. This assumption is reinforced by the way most of us come into contact with the gospels themselves. Although the four gospels are so important as records of what Jesus did and said and of what happened to him, most people only come into contact with the contents of the gospels as small, isolated stories with no clear connection between the various incidents. We rarely read or hear a gospel right through.

This broken contact with the gospels is well illustrated by the traditional readings for the first four Sundays of the Church's year, which are Matthew 24:37-44; Matthew 3:1-12; Matthew 11:2-11 and Matthew 1:18-25. Consequently, it is hard to remember where particular incidents occur within the life and ministry of Jesus. The gospels themselves reinforce this fragmentation of their contents, for when two or more of the four gospels report the same incidents they often place them at different times in Jesus' life. It quickly becomes obvious that the stories existed as separate units of information about Jesus before they were joined together as gospels.

None of this is a hindrance to committed and informed Christians because their faith does not depend on a consistent and clear 'biography' of Jesus. Their belief in God is focused on Jesus because he is God-made-man, the supreme revelation of God, and they relate the various stories about Jesus to their beliefs about him. The stories about Jesus do support what Christians believe about him, but it is also true that the stories make sense to Christians because of what they believe.

This also was the case with the first Christians. They too received their information about Jesus in the form of separate stories. These were told during the private weekly meetings for 'the breaking of bread' (the Eucharist), or as examples given by the apostles and drawn from their recollections of Jesus, to illustrate what they were teaching about him in their public sermons.

The first generation of Christians did not even have the four 'gospels' in the form now familiar to us. Only later were the separate stories woven together into the gospels as we now know them: Matthew, Mark, Luke and John. Most scholars believe that at least thirty years elapsed after the death of Jesus before the first of the gospels as we know them was compiled from the stories circulating about Jesus, and that it may have been as long as seventy years or more before all four were complete.

The theme of the gospels

The collections of teachings, stories and incidents we call 'gospels' are not full accounts of everything Jesus did and said nor of everything that happened to him. They are collections of carefully selected items of information about Jesus, organised round a theme or framework.

Some of these items are parables which Jesus told as he was teaching; some are accounts of confrontations between Jesus and the religious authorities; some are examples of what he taught about such matters as prayer, fasting, how to keep the religious law and what to do about paying taxes. And some are descriptions of miracles performed by Jesus. John's Gospel says that Jesus did many other miracles in the presence of his disciples which are not recorded (Jn 20:30), so the miracles we know about – like all the other items of information we have about Jesus – are only a selection from the many that he did.

The first generations of Christians were taught by the apostles of Jesus who had been with him from the beginning of his public ministry. Those first Christians made sense of the stories about Jesus by relating each of them to the pattern of beliefs taught to them when they were being prepared for baptism. Similarly, a modern reader can only make sense of the gospels by relating their contents to this same pattern of beliefs, the theme, which weaves the contents together.

What, then, is this theme? The answer can be found by turning to the rest of the New Testament, the Acts of the Apostles and the letters. Acts is a history of the thirty years following the ascension of Jesus, and the letters were written by the apostles to the Christian Churches they founded during those years. Because most of this material in the New Testament was written during the time when the gospels themselves were being compiled, it contains valuable evidence for the beliefs about Jesus which lie behind the four gospels. These were the beliefs held by the apostles themselves, who had been with Jesus throughout his ministry, and by the people whom the apostles had taught.

This insight into the beliefs of the earliest Christians is vital for our understanding of the gospels, because these were the very people by whom – and for whom – the four gospels were written, and the gospels reflect their beliefs.

The Acts of the Apostles and the New Testament letters contain three main sources of information about the theme behind the gospels. The first of these sources is the series of reports in Acts of the sermons the apostles preached. The second is provided by the hymns which the first Christians sang, some of which are quoted in the New Testament. The third consists of the summaries of beliefs about Jesus which were taught to people who were being prepared for baptism. Some of these summaries of belief, the earliest form of the Christian creeds, are quoted, particularly in the letters of Paul.

What the apostles proclaimed

The most obvious evidence for the theme behind the gospels is in the Acts of the Apostles, which contains reports of six addresses given by the apostles during the first fifteen years of the church's existence, starting with Peter's address on the day of Pentecost. Acts is by the same author as Luke's Gospel and continues the story from the point where the gospel ends with the ascension of Jesus. Although it was not completed until a generation after the events it describes, there is no reason for modern Christians to doubt that the summaries given by Acts are reliable, for when they were written there were many still alive who could verify them. The references to the apostles' sermons and addresses are:

18

Acts 2:14-39:	Peter to Jewish pilgrims in Jerusalem at Pentecost
Acts 3:13-26:	Peter in the 'Portico of Solomon' at the Temple
Acts 4:10-12:	Peter to the Jewish Great Council, the Sanhedrin
Acts 5:30-32:	Peter to the Great Council, the Sanhedrin, again
Acts 10:36-43:	Peter to Cornelius the centurion and his household
Acts 13:17-41:	Paul in the synagogue at Pisidian Antioch

These reports of addresses and sermons show that the apostles made six points in their preaching about Jesus:

1. Jesus is the saviour promised in the books of the Old Testament, which were 'the scriptures', the record of God's revelation up to the time of Jesus, for the first Christians.

2. The birth, ministry, death and resurrection of Jesus fulfilled the Old Testament promises and brought in the new era of salvation for the whole world.

3. Jesus has ascended to heaven, where he now reigns as Lord of the whole universe.

4. Jesus has sent the Holy Spirit, who is the living proof of the truth of all that Jesus did and taught.

5. Jesus will come again, to complete God's plans for the universe.

6. All can share in this salvation by repenting of their sins, believing in Jesus as the risen Lord and by being baptised.

Although the apostles' sermons and addresses are the most obvious evidence for the beliefs of the first Christians, the other two sources of evidence are equally important: the summaries of belief spoken by candidates for baptism, and the hymns the first Christians sang.

Beliefs for baptism

The second kind of evidence is provided by the summaries of belief which Paul quotes in many of his letters. His readers knew these summaries well, for they themselves had learned such statements of belief during their period of instruction, so that they could repeat them as acts of faith when they were baptised and received as Christians. Paul quotes them to remind his readers of the beliefs he and they all have in common, so that he can draw consequences from them for the Christian way of life.

One of the shortest examples is given by Paul in his Letter to the Romans:

'...if you confess with your lips that Jesus is Lord, and believe in your heart that God raised him from the dead, you will be saved' (Rom 10:9).

A far more extensive example, which may also be an early hymn, occurs in Paul's Letter to the Colossians:

'He (Jesus) is the image of the invisible God,
the first-born of all creation,
for in him all things were created,
in heaven and on earth,
visible and invisible,
whether thrones or dominions or principalities or
    authorities –
all things were created through him and for him.
He is before all things, and in him all things hold
    together,
He is the head of the body, the church;
he is the beginning, the first-born from the dead,

that in everything he might be pre-eminent.
For in him all the fullness of God was pleased to dwell,
and through him to reconcile to himself all things,
whether on earth or in heaven,
making peace by the blood of his cross' (Col 1:15-20).

By making such a statement the Christian converts of this city in Asia Minor were probably being asked to renounce the religious beliefs they previously held, that there were many subordinate gods and that Jesus was only one of them.

Early Christian hymns

The third kind of evidence is to be found in the hymns the first Christians sang at their meetings for worship. As with some modern hymns, passages in the New Testament which look like early hymns are also summaries of belief. The opening verses of John's Gospel might well be such a hymn:

'In the beginning was the Word,
and the Word was with God,
and the Word was God.
He was in the beginning with God;
all things were made through him,
and without him was not anything made that was made.
In him was life,
and the life was the light of men.
The light shines in the darkness,
and the darkness has not overcome it...

And the Word became flesh
and dwelt among us,
full of grace and truth;
we have beheld his glory,
glory as of the only Son from the Father' (Jn 1:1-14).

Hymns are also quoted in other, earlier parts of the New Testament, such as the passage from Colossians quoted above, providing further evidence of the early patterns of belief which the four gospels then expand and illuminate with examples from the life and teaching of Jesus. In his Letter to the Philippians, Paul quotes one of these early hymns about Jesus:

'Who, though he was in the form of God,
did not count equality with God
a thing to be grasped,
but emptied himself,
taking the form of a servant,
being born in the likeness of men.
And being found in human form
he humbled himself
and became obedient unto death
even death on a cross.

Therefore God has highly exalted him
and bestowed on him the name
which is above every name,
that at the name of Jesus
every knee should bow,
in heaven and on earth and under the earth,
and every tongue confess
that Jesus Christ is Lord,
to the glory of God the Father' (Phil 2:6-11).

This hymn would be familiar to Paul's readers, so he quotes it when he urges the Christians in Philippi to take Jesus as their model of humility. But this particular hymn is also an excellent example of a belief-framework for the gospel materials about Jesus. Like John's Gospel, the hymn begins with the status of Jesus before his conception at Nazareth and his birth at Bethlehem, and it continues with his life as a servant through to the crucifixion and resurrection. It concludes with Jesus' ascension and his present status as

Lord of the Universe, the kingdom of the exalted Jesus in which the first Christians believed that they were living. Modern Christians may recognise this ancient hymn as the source for a popular modern hymn, 'At the name of Jesus every knee shall bow'.

Quotations such as these say who Jesus really is, and what he can do for those who believe in him and trust in his saving love. Every story and incident in the four gospels is an illustration of what these beliefs mean, and of their practical consequences for believers in their everyday lives.

All the information about Jesus in the four gospels has been selected and arranged to illustrate this pattern of beliefs about him. If the reader does not relate them to this set of beliefs, the gospel stories lose most of their point. However moving the stories may be, they could merely be about a courageous but unconventional teacher and healer, who went willingly to a horrifying death rather than obey the orders of the religious authorities to modify his teaching and stop healing people. If they are separated from the beliefs that lie behind them, the gospels are not sufficient to establish Jesus as God incarnate, the saviour of humankind.

Verification

When considering the background to the four gospels, it is also important to realise that the first Christians made sense of the gospel stories by relating them to their own baptism and to their worship of God in the 'breaking of bread' – the eucharist. In both of these they believed that they were united with the risen Jesus in all his power; the gospels helped them to understand what this union meant for them in their everyday lives. They met as communities for worship, and recognised that they were united with each other by the union they each of them had with the risen and ascended Jesus.

But they also lived out their lives immersed in the secular world of their time and place, not withdrawn from it, and

23

they confirmed their beliefs about Jesus by applying them to their everyday experiences. They found that the way of life he taught could actually be lived, that they had the power to do it, and this confirmed that his teaching was true and that he really was sharing his risen life with them. Such practical verification of the early beliefs about Jesus is implicit throughout the four gospels, and is central to their credibility.

The gospels proclaim the universal and invincible power of the risen and ascended Jesus to save, in conjunction with the Holy Spirit. But this power is love, so it can only operate fully with the willing response and cooperation of those who are to benefit from it.

The gospels are full of examples of God's power, particularly the miracle stories. But they are also full of examples of human faith, the response to that power by those who put their trust in God. Jesus himself shows that he is truly God, with the power of God to save in all its fullness; but he also shows that he is truly human, by his own faith in the Father who sent him and who raises him from death.

THE MIRACLES

The gospels are the support material for a proclamation of God's saving love, stories about Jesus selected and arranged by four groups of early Christians with different backgrounds. Each gospel contains a selection of information about the life and teaching of Jesus drawn from the experience of his apostles, people who had been with him throughout his public ministry, appointed by Jesus to proclaim to the world the good news of salvation.

In the gospels, Jesus demonstrates that God's love is essentially a relationship with a two-fold pattern of offer and response. God offers the love relationship in all his creative and redeeming power, and invites the free response of trust in his saving power. The miracles selected by the authors of the gospels show the range and power of God's love, and what that love can do for those who respond to him and put their trust in him.

Apart from general summaries of miracles, there are some thirty-six descriptions of specific miracles in the four gospels, including a mention that Jesus had at some time cast devils from Mary Magdalene. Some describe Jesus casting out demons; some are miracles of healing without any mention of demonic possession; three are descriptions of Jesus bringing the dead back to life; and some show Jesus exercising an extraordinary power over nature.

These thirty-six miracles are listed below under these four categories, together with the references to where they occur in each gospel. It is worth noticing that none of the four gospels presents them in the same order as any of the others:

	Matthew	Mark	Luke	John
Demonic Possession				
A blind and dumb man	12:22			
The Canaanite woman's daughter	15:21-28	7:24-30		
A dumb man	9:32-33		11:14	
The epileptic boy	17:14-17	9:14-21	9:37-43	
The man or men in Gadara	8:28-34	5:1-20	8:26-39	
(Mary Magdalene		16:9	8:2)	
The man in a synagogue in Capernaum		1:23-28	4:33-37	
The woman bent double in a synagogue			13:10-17	
Healings with no mention of demons				
Blind Bartimaeus	20:29-34	10:46-52	18:35-43	
A blind man at Bethsaida		8:22-26		
A blind man born blind				9:1-7
Two blind men	9:27-31			
The centurion's servant	8:5-13		7:1-10	
A deaf-mute		7:31-37		

	Matthew	Mark	Luke	John
A dropsical man			14:1-6	
A leper	8:1-4	1:40-45	5:12-16	
Ten lepers			17:11-19	
Peter's mother-in-law	8:14-15	1:29-31	4:38-39	
A paralysed man in Capernaum	9:1-8	2:1-12	5:17-26	
A paralysed man at the pool of Bethesda				5:1-9
The high priest's slave			22:50-51	
The son of an official at Capernaum				4:46-54
A man with a withered hand	12:9-14	3:1-6	6:6-11	
A woman with an issue of blood	9:20-22	5:23-34	8:43-48	

Raising the dead

	Matthew	Mark	Luke	John
Jairus's daughter	9:18-26	5:21-43	8:40-56	
Lazarus				11:1-44
A widow's son at Nain			7:11-17	

Nature miracles

	Matthew	Mark	Luke	John
A great catch of fish			5:4-10	
A catch of fish				21:6-11
The coin in a fish's mouth	17:24-27			
Feeding the 5000	14:13-21	6:30-44	9:10-17	6:1-14
Feeding the 4000	15:32-39	8:1-10		
A fig tree cursed	21:19	11:14,20		
The storm stilled	8:23-27	4:35-41	8:22-25	
Walking on water	14:22-33	6:45-52		6:16-21
Water changed to wine				2:1-11

Each of these miracles will be examined later in more detail, and then there will be suggestions about the way they serve the main themes of Christian belief which the gospel material illustrates.

Faith

Jesus could apparently do very little for people who would not trust him and had no faith in his powers to help them. Indeed, when he returned to Nazareth, the small town where he had grown up, Jesus 'marvelled because of their unbelief' in him, and he was only able to help one or two of the people there. His reputation as a teacher and healer had gone before him and at first his old neighbours were astonished at his wisdom when he taught in their synagogue. Then they took offence because they thought he had grown arrogant: 'Is not this the carpenter, the son of Mary and brother of James and Joses and Judas and Simon...?' (Mk 6:2-6). One of the gospels says that they even tried to kill him when he rebuked them (Lk 4:23). The gospels make it clear that Jesus would not impose miracles of healing on people without their cooperation, no matter how much he knew that they needed him. Many of the accounts of the miracles emphasise the faith of people, both of the people who directly benefit and of their friends and relations. A leper tells Jesus that if he wants to he can make him clean; the woman with a long history of uncured haemorrhaging believes that she will be healed if she merely touches his cloak; blind Bartimaeus insists on calling out to Jesus when the crowd tries to silence him. Jesus tells them that their faith has healed them.

On some occasions he draws on the faith of the healthy when healing the sick. Four men lower their friend through a hole in the roof to get him to Jesus; Jesus notices their faith and first forgives their friend his sins, then heals him. Jesus marvels at the faith of the centurion who believes that Jesus can heal his servant without going to the house where he lies sick. A woman from Phoenicia believes that he can heal her daughter lying many miles away in Tyre. Some bring a deaf-mute to Jesus, others a blind man, and beg Jesus to heal them. Questioned by Jesus, the father of an epileptic boy answers that he does indeed have faith that Jesus can heal his son where the apostles have failed, but he fears that his faith is insufficient for the boy's needs; Jesus reassures him and heals the boy.

The clue to this is, again, the nature of love. God's initiative of love requires the free response of faith for it to be effective. The power of God's love itself confers the freedom to respond in love. And without such a free response the love of God cannot be effective.

As in other gospel material, many of the miracle stories demonstrate this fundamental love pattern of initiative and response, in which faith is such an essential ingredient. It was a point of great practical importance for the first Christians, and has remained so ever since. As the rest of the New Testament also testifies, the love of God is universally available without any question of race, gender, age, social class or even of religious heritage. But it is not imposed on anyone; it can only be effective where there is at least some measure of response in love.

3

Nature miracles

Miracle	Matthew	Mark	Luke	John
Water changed to wine				2:1-11
The great catch of fish			5:4-10	
The storm stilled	8:23-27	4:35-41	8:22-25	
Feeding the 5000	14:13-21	6:30-44	9:10-17	6:1-14
Walking on water	14:22-33	6:45-52		6:16-21
Feeding the 4000	15:32-39	8:1-10		
The coin in a fish's mouth	17:24-27			
A fig tree cursed	21:18-22	11:12-14, 20-24		
Another catch of fish				21:6-11

As we have seen, the beliefs of the first Christians about Jesus were based on the preaching and teaching of the apostles, the inner group of disciples of Jesus who had been with him throughout his public ministry and after his resurrection. The apostles illustrated these beliefs with collections of incidents from the life of Jesus which were eventually arranged and edited to form the four gospels.

These early beliefs about Jesus included his pre-existence before his conception and birth; they continued with his earthly life and death; and they reached on beyond his resurrection and ascension. The first Christians believed that before his conception and birth, even before the creation of the universe, Jesus Christ was already Son of God – however difficult this may be for the human imagination.

John's Gospel opens with the great assertion that Jesus is the 'word' of God, the 'logos'. This means that he was the divine agent of creation. In the opening chapter of Genesis, on which the opening of John's Gospel is modelled, the whole process of creation is like an omnipotent sovereign issuing commands which systematically bring the universe into existence. Using this model, John's Gospel presents Jesus as the Son of God who shared in God's original work of creation by relaying God's commands. He is the Word of God and therefore the words he utters during his life on earth have all the authority of God to give life and light to the world:

'In the beginning was the Word,
and the Word was with God,
and the Word was God.
He was in the beginning with God;
all things were made through him,
and without him was not anything made that was made.
In him was life,
and the life was the light of men.
The light shines in the darkness,
and the darkness has not overcome it' (Jn 1:1-5).

When the divine and omnipotent Word became incarnate as Jesus of Nazareth, the beliefs continue, he laid aside the infinite and eternal attributes of God and entered his creation as a man. He was virginally conceived by Mary in Nazareth and born at Bethlehem after the normal human period of gestation. In the words of an early Christian hymn, as we have already noted, he did not cling to his divine equality:

'but emptied himself,
taking the form of a servant,
being born in the likeness of men.
And being found in human form
he humbled himself
and became obedient unto death,
even death on a cross' (Phil 2:7-8).

Beliefs such as these lie behind the nature miracles, which are glimpses, like the transfiguration, of the other 'nature' of Jesus, the divinity voluntarily hidden or relinquished at his incarnation. Once again, the problem lies with the human imagination rather than with the beliefs themselves. We have no means of visualising what it means to be divine; we can only use concepts taken from human experience and extend them beyond their original meaning, so that they can help us to speak about the divine mystery revealed by Jesus.

The four gospels between them record a number of miracles in which Jesus showed that he had powers which go beyond the limits of the 'laws' of nature. They serve as signs to indicate the power which is present in all expressions of God's saving love. According to the gospels and Christian beliefs, this is the same power which brought the universe into existence and continues to sustain it. Jesus was the living expression of this saving love of God, the divine initiative of love made accessible to all, inviting trust and loving response from the world he had come to save.

The water changed to wine (Jn 2:1-11)

According to John's Gospel, Jesus performed the first of all his miracles at a wedding feast in Cana of Galilee to save the people from the embarrassment of running short of wine. Presumably they were family friends or relatives, for Jesus' mother had been invited and may even have been involved in helping to organise it. Jesus went as well, together with some of the people who had already begun to accompany him and assist him in his ministry.

When the wine ran out Mary told Jesus, 'They have no wine.' Her remark may have meant no more than a request for Jesus and his friends to see if they could get more, but Jesus interpreted it as a suggestion – or even a command – that he should do something extraordinary about it.

Jesus replied, 'O woman, what have you to do with me? My hour has not yet come' (Jn 2:4). Jesus here used a particularly solemn and formal mode of address to his mother, and he went on to tell her that her authority over him as her son had ended. Everything he does from now on will be directly related to his messianic mission, and it is not yet the time to make this obvious to everyone.

Nevertheless, Jesus took charge behind the scenes at the wedding feast and ordered the servants to fill six great stone storage jars with water. Normally they held the water for the ritual ablutions the Jewish religious laws required in every home, and each jar held twenty or thirty gallons.

When the jars were full, Jesus told the servants to draw from their contents and carry it into the feast. They did so, and found that they were carrying wine. These servants were the only people other than Jesus who knew where the wine had come from. The surprised president of the wedding feast made a point of congratulating the bridegroom on the quality of the newly-arrived wine. It wasn't usual, he said, to delay serving the best wine until late in the feast when the guests had already drunk freely.

John's Gospel concludes its account of the incident by pointing out that this was the first of the 'signs' performed by Jesus. It adds that Jesus disciples recognised it as a manifestation of his 'glory' and that they believed in him.

John calls Jesus' miracles 'signs' in other passages also. They are signs – for those who have faith – of who he really is, and this gospel explains why they are recorded (Jn 20:30-31). But Jesus will not perform miracles merely to convince people that he is the Son of God. They must trust him, have confidence in him, accept that they have need of him and be prepared to be changed by him. Then the miracles become revelations which can deepen their faith and their understanding. If they are suspicious of him or antagonistic Jesus will not work miracles just to convince them that they are mistaken.

The signs indicate who Jesus really is, but they also point forward to his crucifixion and resurrection; the gospel stories were told, shaped and selected after the resurrection so they are full of significant hindsights. Jesus turned the water into wine, water used in the Jewish purification rituals. When the first Christians looked back at this incident they could see that it pointed to the perfect purification that Jesus had made possible, not just for Jews but for all peoples.

This significance is reinforced by the next incident recorded in John's Gospel, when Jesus 'purified' the great Jewish temple in Jerusalem by driving out the traders. He said then, in cryptic words which only became clear to his disciples after his resurrection, that he could rebuild the temple in three days. He himself, risen from the dead, would be the new temple for all humankind.

His disciples later realised that the miracle at the wedding feast in Cana had been their first glimpse of Jesus' 'glory', the word the Hebrews used for that power of God's saving presence which had led them from their slavery in Egypt at the Exodus, and which they believed now dwelt amongst them in the temple in Jerusalem. Whether or not they had been Jews, the first Christians incorporated those Jewish beliefs into their beliefs about Jesus.

The great catch of fish (Lk 5:4-10)

The gospels provide no information about Jesus from the age of twelve, when he surprised the scholars of the temple in Jerusalem with his wisdom, until he was about thirty-three years of age, when he began his public ministry in Galilee.

He might have spent those 'hidden' years just quietly working in Joseph's carpenter's shop in Nazareth. He could also have travelled anywhere in the Mediterranean world and beyond along the network of Roman roads, or have taken passage in the great ships which traded from the Lebanese ports of Tyre and Sidon and from Alexandria at the mouth of the River Nile. Within Palestine itself he had ample opportunity to visit Jewish religious communities, such as the one at Qumran near the head of the Dead Sea now famous for the discovery nearby of the 'Dead Sea scrolls'.

As the time drew near to begin his public ministry Jesus began to make himself known to the kind of people in the Galilee area who might help him and learn from him. After his baptism and the temptations, he toured the synagogues of Galilee teaching and performing acts of exorcism and healing. His reputation rapidly grew and crowds began to follow him, even though the people of Nazareth, where he had grown up, rejected him because they thought he was making blasphemous claims.

From these followers Jesus selected the inner group who would become 'the twelve', the disciples who remained with him throughout his ministry. Jesus chose the first four from the fishermen of Capernaum where he had established his base. His invitation for them to join him came immediately after he had performed a miracle for them.

A large crowd had gathered round Jesus on the shore of the Sea of Galilee, so Jesus boarded a fishing boat belonging to Simon Peter and Andrew. He then taught the crowd from the boat. Simon knew Jesus well, because Jesus had cured his mother-in-law of a fever in Simon's house in Capernaum.

When he had finished teaching, Jesus asked Simon to take the boat into deeper water and begin fishing. Simon protested that he and his partners had fished all night without success, but he agreed to do what Jesus asked. When they let down the nets they caught so many fish that the nets began to break and they had to call for help from another boat belonging to James and John. They filled both of the boats so full of fish that they began to sink.

Simon seems to have been the first to recognise that their catch was miraculous, for he knelt before Jesus in the boat and begged him to go away, 'for I am a sinful man, O Lord' (Lk 5:8). Simon's reaction to Jesus was similar to the reaction of the prophet Isaiah when he had a vision of God's majesty in the temple (Is 6:5); Isaiah had also expressed his sinfulness and unworthiness before God. Jesus reassured Simon and the others with him, 'Do not be afraid; henceforth you will be catching men' (Lk 5:10). When they had hauled their boats ashore the four men left everything and followed Jesus.

John's Gospel records a similar miracle after the resurrection of Jesus when the disciples returned to their fishing. Some commentators think they are two versions of the same incident, even though they are set so far apart in the life of Jesus. There are many differences between the two accounts but in both gospels the catch of fish symbolises what Jesus expects of his disciples. Here in Luke, the miraculous catch of fish at the opening of his ministry emphasises the assistance they are to give Jesus during his public ministry; in John the miracle emphasises the responsibility Jesus lays on the disciples to carry on his mission after his ascension.

The stilling of the storm (Mt 8:23-27; Mk 4:35-41; Lk 8:22-25)

A little later in his Galilean ministry, Jesus again found himself on the shores of the Sea of Galilee near Capernaum, surrounded by crowds. They had crowded to him in the town, bringing the sick and people in need of exorcism, and in the evening they had followed him to the lakeside. He was exhausted.

Perhaps just to escape from the crowds which thronged him, or perhaps to extend his work, Jesus decided to cross to the other side of the Sea of Galilee. Touchingly, the account says that his fishermen disciples 'took him with them, just as he was' (Mk 4:36), after they had sent away the multitude. The gospels give the impression that Jesus was utterly spent. As his disciples rowed he fell asleep on the helmsman's seat in the stern of the boat.

Suddenly they found themselves caught in one of the storms for which the Sea of Galilee is notorious, and as the disciples struggled with their swamping boat they woke Jesus and called urgently for him to help them manage the boat. Jesus rebuked the wind and commanded the sea to be still, as if they were personal forces. The wind ceased, the waves died away and they were floating peacefully in a great calm. 'Why are you afraid?' Jesus asked his disciples, 'Have you no faith?' (Mk 4:39).

Clearly, the disciples had not expected a miracle, for all three gospel accounts end with them expressing fear and surprise. 'Who then is this,' they asked, 'that even wind and sea obey him?' (Mk 4:41).

For the Jewish disciples of Jesus and for the early Christians this miracle would have echoes of the story of the creation of the universe at the beginning of the Book of Genesis. That opening chapter of the Bible depicts God creating by stilling the chaotic storm of primeval forces and then separating light from darkness, heaven from earth and water from land. Day by day, the process is extended until the whole creation is a single, ordered system in which every aspect of it is good.

Whatever happened in the storm-tossed boat on the Sea of Galilee, his disciples began to realise that Jesus had powers similar to those which had brought the world into existence. The experience made it easier for them to recognise that everything he did was evidence of an underlying power and pattern. He brought order from chaos, and prevented evil from turning it into chaos again.

When his disciples looked back on this miracle after the crucifixion and resurrection of Jesus, it would help them to understand what had really been happening to Jesus and what his death and resurrection meant for the renewal of creation. It would also be a reassuring incident to recount to the first Christians, to show them what Jesus could do for them when they feared that their lives were at the mercy of destructive demonic forces which mere human power could not control.

Feeding the 5000 (Mt 14:13-21; Mk 6:30-44; Lk 9:10-17; Jn 6:1-14)

The feeding of the 5000 is the only miracle recorded in all four gospels, an indication of the importance attached to it by the early Christians in all of the different locations for which the gospels were written.

Still in Galilee, Jesus had by this time selected the twelve disciples from the many people who were following him, and he had sent the twelve out in pairs to go through the villages of Galilee preaching and healing. They had returned with reports of their success.

News of the remarkable events associated with Jesus and his disciples also reached Herod Antipas, the son of Herod the Great appointed by Rome to be the Jewish ruler of Galilee. He had executed Jesus' cousin, John the Baptist, at the request of his step-daughter, Salome, after she had danced for him at a banquet, and presented her with John's head.

Jesus was making powerful enemies and it is little wonder that he and his disciples again needed to get away, to escape from the crowds and to find time for reflection and prayer. But many people saw Jesus going and followed him, so Jesus preached to them in the remote place where they found him.

When evening came and the crowds showed no sign of dispersing, the disciples asked Jesus to send the people away to buy food for themselves. Jesus told his disciples that they themselves should get food for the crowd. Philip pointed out that food to the value of two hundred days' wages would not be enough, so Jesus asked them what food there was. Andrew answered, perhaps with some sarcasm, that there was a boy there with five small bread rolls and two fish. Jesus told the disciples to organise the crowd into groups and get them to sit down.

Jesus then took the bread rolls and the fishes, raised his eyes to heaven in blessing, broke the food into pieces and gave them to the disciples to distribute to the crowd. Everyone was fed, and there was enough food left over to fill twelve baskets.

When he took the food, blessed it and shared it out, Jesus was following the normal Jewish custom for the start of a formal meal. But his actions also became the pattern of the Christian communion meal, 'the breaking of bread' or 'eucharist', which was the main form of worship for the first

Christian communities and has remained so for Christians ever since. This is one reason why this miracle is in all four gospels.

In John's gospel the story of the miracle is followed by a long report of a discussion next day in Capernaum between Jesus and some of the people who had been present. The discussion rapidly turned into an argument. Jesus accused them of following him because he could meet their material needs; they must believe, he said, that he himself was the bread of life come down from heaven, sent by the Father to feed them and give life to the world.

Some of his listeners were from Nazareth and had known Jesus as a boy. 'How does he now say, I have come down from heaven?' they asked (Jn 6:42).

Jesus pressed them further. 'I am the living bread come down from heaven; if anyone eats this bread, he will live for ever; and the bread which I shall give for the life of the world is my flesh' (Jn 6:51).

This indeed baffled the crowd, and Jesus continued further still, so that they could have no doubts about his claims: 'Unless you eat the flesh of the Son of man and drink his blood, you have no life in you' (Jn 6:53). They must eat his flesh and drink his blood, he told them, so that they could abide in him and he in them.

As Jesus made increasingly strong claims for himself, the crowd faded away until only his twelve closest disciples were left. Jesus asked them if they too were leaving him. 'To whom shall we go?' answered Peter. 'You have the words of eternal life' (Jn 6:68).

The twelve disciples were as baffled as the crowd, but they accepted what Jesus said because it fitted in with other things they had heard him say and seen him do, and they had faith in him. Eventually, Jesus' words and actions at the last supper, followed by his crucifixion and the resurrection, would all confirm the truth of what Jesus had said. As apostles, the twelve would later report these words of Jesus to the first Christians to explain what they were doing in the eucharist and why it must be the centre of their Christian life.

Walking on water (Mt 14:22-33; Mk 6:45-52; Lk 6:16-21)

The scene of this miracle is very early morning with Jesus on the western side of the Sea of Galilee and his disciples in a boat somewhere out on the waters. The previous evening, after the miraculous feeding of the 5000, Jesus had sent the disciples across to Bethsaida, east of Capernaum, while he stayed to placate the crowd. The people he had fed wanted Jesus to let them make him their king, and Jesus had to convince them that he must refuse because he could not be the kind of king they wanted. The crowd finally dispersed and Jesus climbed a nearby hill to find solitude for prayer.

As the sun began to rise over the Sea of Galilee, Jesus saw the boat silhouetted against the light with the disciples still rowing hard against a strong wind. Suddenly, the disciples saw Jesus walking on the water alongside their boat. Thinking it was an apparition they screamed in terror, but Jesus hastened to reassure them that there was nothing to be frightened about.

When he realised it really was Jesus, Peter asked if he could join him on the water, and Jesus told him to come. Peter stepped over the side of the boat on to the water and began to walk, but his nerve failed and he started to sink. Jesus caught him, both of them climbed into the boat and the wind died away.

It is a strange event, and some scholars have suggested that it belongs to the period between the resurrection of Jesus and his ascension, when the gospels record similar incidents, but the disciples' terror and Peter's impetuosity help to make it convincing. Whenever it happened, it was more than a mere passing illusion caused by Jesus wading in shallow waters close inshore.

Jesus rebuked the disciples for their momentary terror, and reminded them about the recent miracle when he had fed five thousand people. They should not have been surprised, he implied, considering the other things they had seen him do.

Like the miracle when Jesus calmed the storm on the

same stretch of water, the incident has echoes of the account of creation of the world in the opening chapter of the Book of Genesis. That description of the creation reads, '...darkness was upon the face of the deep, and the Spirit of God was moving over the face of the waters' (Gen 1:2). It would remind the disciples of the Exodus, the escape from Egypt when God led the Hebrews across the waters to freedom and safety.

Later in their lives, the disciples would recall this incident as further evidence of who it really was who had been crucified and risen from the dead, and an indication of what his crucifixion and resurrection really achieved. The gospels show that they included it in their own teaching to the first Christians. It was important for them to realise that Jesus was far more than a rabbi or teacher, even an outstandingly impressive one; he had been sent by God to share with them his invincible power to save.

Feeding the 4000 (Mt 15:32-39; Mk 8:1-10)

Some think that this miracle is another version of the feeding of the 5000, but this is unlikely because it is recorded in two of the gospels which also contain the earlier miracle. Even so, it is still a possible theory, because the gospel stories circulated widely and separately amongst the first Christians before they were recorded in the gospels as we now have them.

There are clear differences between the two sets of stories, however, which suggest that they tell of different miracles. In this miracle the crowd had been with Jesus and his disciples for three days, not just one day, and the disciples knew that they still had some food left for them – loaves and dried fish – even if it was inadequate to feed them all. This time, according to Mark's Gospel, Jesus blessed the bread and the fish separately, and there were seven baskets of fragments left over, not twelve as before.

They were again in a remote place, perhaps because

Jesus was finding that his teaching was regularly disrupted by hostile heckling from members of established religious groups. Jesus was moved with compassion by the crowd's hunger for food, just as he had been moved by the earlier crowd's hunger for leadership, and he would not just send them away.

Jesus took the seven loaves his disciples had with them and the few fish. Then he blessed and broke the bread and told the disciples to distribute it, and blessed the fish and handed that over for distribution. When everyone was satisfied the disciples gathered up the scraps and filled seven baskets with them.

The miracle shows the same eucharistic pattern of taking, blessing, breaking and distributing as the earlier one, with the same kind of significance that Jesus had pointed out in the discourse which follows the earlier miracle in John's gospel. But this time, as a result of a dispute with Pharisees, Jesus referred his disciples to another aspect of the two miracles.

The confrontation occurred shortly after the miracle, immediately after Jesus and the disciples had crossed to another shore of the Sea of Galilee. Some Pharisees demanded that he give them 'a sign from heaven' as proof of his claims. Jesus answered them, as he had in a previous confrontation (Mt 12:40), that the only sign they would get was 'the sign of Jonah'. Jonah had spent three days and nights in the belly of the whale, and this was later seen by Christians as a symbol of the death and resurrection of Jesus.

The disciples and Jesus again took to their boat, and the disciples told him that they had only brought one loaf of bread with them. With the Pharisees in mind, Jesus replied by warning them of the 'leaven' – the yeast which spreads through bread dough – of the official religious teachers. The disciples continued to worry about the shortage of bread, so Jesus told them to remember the number of baskets of scraps in the two miracles, twelve and seven respectively.

In Jewish and early Christian number symbolism, twelve

referred to the Jews and seven to the Gentiles, the rest of the nations of the world. By this way of thinking, the two miracles indicated that Jesus provided enough 'bread' to feed the whole world, Jews and Gentiles alike. The disciples' worries, Jesus told them, showed that they did not understand what he was really doing.

The coin in a fish's mouth (Mt 17:24-27)

The miracle of the coin in the fish's mouth is Jesus' way of meeting a tax demand, but it is not clear which of the many taxes was involved, whether a religious tax levied on all Jews for the upkeep of the temple, one levied by the Jewish civil authorities or a Roman tax. The tax collector in Capernaum approached Peter about Jesus' tax, and Jesus told Peter that rulers do not tax their own sons: 'the sons are free' (Mt 17:26). This comment suggests that it was the Temple tax, and as Son of God Jesus did not feel obliged to help pay the costs of his Father's house.

Jesus paid up to avoid giving offence, not because he was obliged to pay, but his method of obtaining the money to pay was itself a demonstration of who he was. He told Peter to go fishing and he would find the necessary amount both for Jesus and for himself in the mouth of the first fish he caught. The gospel account ends without saying whether the miracle actually occurred, but it certainly implies that it did. Later, when the Pharisees and Herodians tried to trap Jesus with a question about taxes, he pointed to a Roman coin and told them that they had no problem about reconciling their religious and secular loyalties when they spent the Roman money (Mt 22:15-22).

Despite the antagonism of the Jewish authorities towards Jesus, and his own fierce criticisms of them, there is no instance anywhere in the gospels of Jesus refusing his obligations to pay the legal taxes. Nor does he ever even criticise the Roman authorities who controlled Palestine in his day. Jesus gave no support to people who wanted him to lend his authority to religious or nationalistic movements dedicated to opposing the ruling powers.

The miracle would be an important lesson for the early Christians when they had to decide whether they should obey non-Christian religious and civil authorities. Under the guidance of the apostles they did obey unless – as in acts of emperor worship – it involved an explicit denial of the supreme authority of God as revealed by Jesus Christ. Paul was clear about the matter, perhaps because he himself had Roman citizenship, and he told the Christians of Rome that they should be subject to rulers as authorities appointed by God, and pay the taxes they levied (Rom 13:1-17).

A fig tree cursed (Mt 21:18-22; Mk 11:12-14,20-24)

The cursing of a fig tree by Jesus during his last week in Jerusalem is one of the strangest and most difficult of all the miracles, for it is the only one where Jesus destroys something because he seems to have been unreasonably disappointed.

As Jesus and the disciples returned to Jerusalem from nearby Bethany, where they were lodging for the Passover, Jesus saw a fig tree in full leaf and looked for fruit on it. He found none because it was not yet time for it to fruit, so Jesus cursed it. Either immediately (Matthew) or next day (Mark) the disciples found that the fig tree was dead and withered.

The two gospels which record this incident place it within the immediate context of Jesus clearing the traders out of the Temple courts and declaring that the Jews had allowed it to become a den of robbers. This may not account for Jesus cursing the fig tree, but it does help to explain why the incident became a symbol of the failure of the Jewish religion. Eight centuries earlier the prophet Hosea had used the image of a fig tree to condemn the way the Hebrew people treated their God. He said that God hoped that Israel would be like the first fruit on the fig tree, but they had deserted him for pagan religions dedicated to material power and became detestable (Hos 9:10).

The early Christians would be familiar with Hosea's comments as part of 'the scriptures'.

By the end of the week in which the fig tree died the highest Jewish religious authorities had finally rejected Jesus and manoeuvred the Roman magistrate into executing him. For Christians it was a further and more terrible example of Hosea's condemnation of Hebrew religious institutions under the figure of a fig tree. The very first Christians were all Jews who continued to practice their Jewish faith (Acts 2:46), but they broke with it within twenty years of the death of Jesus as the leaders of their old Hebrew religion became more hostile towards them, and as more and more Gentiles became Christians.

Another catch of fish (Jn 21:6-11)

After the appearances of the risen Jesus to the disciples in the upper room in Jerusalem, Matthew's and John's Gospels record that the disciples returned to Galilee. In Matthew they went to the Mount of the Transfiguration where Jesus had first appointed them; in John they returned to their trade of fishing on the Sea of Galilee; both gospels state that Jesus appeared to them there. There is plenty of time for both of these Galilean incidents during the period between the resurrection of Jesus and his ascension forty days later.

In John's Gospel the Galilean visit of the risen Jesus to his disciples is the occasion for a miraculous catch of fish, similar to the miracle Luke reports when Jesus first began to ask disciples to follow him in Galilee (Lk 5:4-10). Seven of the eleven disciples remaining from the twelve (Judas had hanged himself) had spent the night in a boat fishing but had caught nothing. As dawn broke a man standing on the shore called out to ask if they had caught anything. Without realising that it was Jesus, they replied that they had caught nothing. Jesus told them to cast their nets on the starboard side of the boat, and when they did so they caught so many fish that the net was too heavy to haul aboard.

'The disciple whom Jesus loved' – traditionally John – realised who it was and said to Peter, 'It is the Lord!' (Jn 21:7). Peter, who was naked, tied a garment about himself and jumped overboard to wade the hundred yards to the shore. The others made for the shore in the boat, towing the net, where they found that Jesus had brought bread with him and was cooking fish on a fire he had lit. He told Peter to fetch some of the fish they had caught and invited them all to eat. John's Gospel says that the catch totalled 153 fish, a precise number which may indicate that this report was written by someone who was present and remembered the details.

After they had eaten, Jesus three times asked Peter if he loved him, and Peter replied with increasing vehemence that he did. After each reply Jesus told Peter to feed his sheep or to look after his lambs. The series of three questions and commissions reverse Peter's three-fold denial of Jesus reported earlier in the gospel (Jn 18:17,25,27), and reinforce his role as chief of the apostles.

The miracle and the commission to Peter help to round off the structure of John's Gospel and provide it with a fitting conclusion. The gospel opens with a massive affirmation that Jesus was the creative power of God made incarnate. It ends with a miracle which indicates that the missionary work of the apostles will be only successful through divine power rather than by any human effort.

The significance of the nature miracles

Between them, the nine nature miracles in the four gospels are a powerful statement about the kind of power Jesus was able to command and who he really was. They are records of miraculous events, but they also indicate how humble Jesus was. Despite possessing such divine powers as Son of God, Jesus allowed himself to be born a human being and to pass through childhood and early manhood. He accepted human frailties in the way he conducted his public ministry, and he willingly submitted to the suffering which culminated in his crucifixion.

These miracles further indicate the nature of the power still at work in the world in the Christian communities. The power which brought the world into existence, which continued to sustain it, was also the power of God's redeeming love available to all.

The walking on water and stilling of the storm echo the actions of God in the description of the creation of the universe in the opening chapter of the Book of Genesis, and the Exodus from Egypt, the fundamental act of redemption for the Hebrew religion.

The two miraculous feedings of crowds point to the ritual acts of taking, blessing, breaking and distributing bread in the Christian sacred meal, the eucharist.

The two miraculous catches of fish emphasise that the success of Jesus' mission to the world will be achieved under divine direction and by divine power rather than by human effort. That one of these miracles occurred at the beginning of his ministry in Galilee, and the other after his resurrection, indicated to the first Christians that the mission of Jesus was being continued by the apostles.

Even the coin in the fish's mouth and the cursing of the fig tree were relevant to the first Christians as they applied the life and teaching of Jesus to their own situations. Being Christians did not release them from their worldly responsibilities nor their obedience to worldly authorities; they should fulfil their obligations even if only to avoid unnecessary scandal, just as Jesus had done.

But the first Christians also had to think out their relationship to the Hebrew religion in which most of them had been reared. The religious leaders had rejected Jesus claim to be the Christ – the long-awaited Messiah. Relations with the Jewish authorities became more strained as the apostles reaffirmed that claim, and the strain increased as growing numbers of Gentiles became Christians. The fig tree had failed to produce fruit when it was unexpectedly required of it, and the Hebrew religious institutions had failed to provide the liberating power God had intended. Christians began to think of themselves as the new Israel, the people of the new covenant which now replaced the old one and which would succeed where the old one had failed.

4

Resurrection miracles

Miracle	Matthew	Mark	Luke	John
The son of a widow at Nain			7:11-17	
Jairus' daughter	9:18-26	5:21-43	8:40-56	
Lazarus				11:1-44

As the gospels all reach their climax with the resurrection of Jesus from the dead after his crucifixion, it seems surprising that they only contain three reports of miracles in which Jesus brought dead people back to life again. The obvious explanation might be that Jesus only brought three people back to life again during his public ministry, but this is unconvincing because the gospels themselves state that they only contain a small selection of the miracles Jesus did.

It is worth remembering that Jesus did not come for the sake of doing miracles, particularly miracles in which he brought people back to life only for them to die again. He repeatedly refused to perform miracles when his opponents demanded proofs of his claims, and he seldom did them to deepen the faith of his followers. He came to bring forgiveness and to reconcile the world to God, so that death would lead to eternal life. Above all, he came to reveal and express the invincible love of God which nothing could thwart, particularly death. The miracles are always subordinate to these objectives.

Like the exorcisms and the other healing miracles, all

three of the resurrection miracles are expressions of Jesus' compassion for people in need, and this may be a more helpful as well as a more simple explanation of why he did them.

In two of the three reported cases of Jesus raising people after they had died, they were untimely deaths of young people. In one case the young person died while Jesus was on his way to heal her; in another a young man's death left his widowed mother without means of support. In the far more complex case of Lazarus, he and his two sisters were close friends of Jesus and Jesus first received a message that Lazarus was ill, not dead. However, before Jesus set out for the village near Jerusalem where Lazarus had lived he did tell his disciples that Lazarus had in fact died.

The son of a widow at Nain (Lk 7:11-17)

The first occasion when Jesus brought a dead person to life again, according to the sequence of events in the gospels, occurred in Galilee at the small town of Nain. Jesus had grown up a few miles north of Nain at Nazareth. As Jesus and his disciples drew near to the entrance of the town a funeral procession was just leaving, accompanied by a large crowd. The dead man was the only son of a widow who was thus left with no means of support. The woman was distraught.

Jesus told the mother of the dead man not to weep; then he went to where the body was being carried on a bier and touched it. The men carrying it stopped. Jesus said, 'Young man, I say to you, arise' (Lk 7:14), and the dead man sat up and began to speak. Jesus told his mother to take him.

Naturally, the crowd was amazed, and Luke reports that they began to shout that a great prophet had arisen among them – Jesus had spent his childhood within five miles of the place – and that God had visited his people.

Immediately after this incident Luke reports the arrival of messengers from John the Baptist, who had been imprisoned by the Jewish ruler of Galilee, Herod Antipas. John had heard of the growing reputation of Jesus and he had sent to ask if Jesus really was 'he who is to come'.

While John's messengers were with Jesus they saw him healing and exorcising people brought to him. Jesus told them to tell John about the remarkable things they had seen Jesus do, including 'the dead are raised up' (Lk 7:22). But it is significant that the climax of the list of wonders is 'the poor have good news preached to them' (Lk 7:22). The miracles are always subordinate to this primary objective of Jesus' mission.

Anyone familiar with the stories of the prophet Elijah – and that would indeed include all the Jews present at this miracle at Nain – would recall the incident when the prophet restored to life the dead son of a widow at Zarephath (1 Kings 17:10-24). In Hebrew tradition, Elijah would return to announce the arrival of the Messiah. The crowd at Nain at least thought that Jesus was the new Elijah. Perhaps John the Baptist had wanted to be reassured that Jesus was greater than Elijah and was the Messiah himself.

Jairus' daughter (Mt 9:18-26; Mk 5:21-43; Lk 8:40-56)

Early in his Galilean ministry Jesus and his disciples had crossed to the southern end of the Sea of Galilee to the Decapolis, a non-Jewish region where Jesus exorcised a raving demoniac living among the tombs. After that miracle the local people had begged them to leave, so they had returned to Galilee again.

As they arrived back a crowd gathered round Jesus; a prominent local Jew named Jairus, the president of a synagogue, shouldered his way through. He fell at Jesus' feet and begged him to come and lay his hands on his small daughter, for she was at the point of death. Surrounded by the crowd, Jesus set out for the man's house.

On the way Jesus was delayed when a woman with a chronic haemorrhage approached him from behind and touched his cloak in the hope that the action might heal her. Aware of what had happened, Jesus asked who had touched him; the woman came forward fearfully and Jesus told her that her faith had made her whole again.

During the delay, someone from Jairus' house arrived to say that his daughter had died and Jesus need not be troubled any further. There is a hint here that they thought that Jesus had failed as a healer. Despite this message, Jesus told Jairus not to fear and to have faith. Then he told the crowd to stay behind and, taking with him only Peter, James and John of the disciples, he went on with Jairus into the house.

Inside the house Jesus found a scene of despair with the household loudly bewailing the girl's death. He assured them all, despite their derision, that the girl was only sleeping, then he sent all the household outside except for the dead girl's parents. In his native Aramaic language Jesus told the twelve-year-old girl to get up – literally, to rise – and she immediately did so and began to walk about. They were all so astonished that Jesus had to remind them to give her something to eat.

Was the girl really dead or only in a deep coma? The depth of anguish and mourning Jesus found in the household, their derision when he said that she was only sleeping, and their subsequent astonishment all suggest that she had indeed died while Jesus was on his way to her.

Mark and Luke's gospels both say that Jesus ordered everyone to tell no one what he had done for the girl. Jesus made a similar request after a number of his miracles. He was anxious that people should accept him on his own terms and his own understanding of what the Messiah should be like, not because he performed miracles or fitted the popular idea of a nationalist Messiah. Those terms would eventually include the crucifixion, and even his closest disciples had grave difficulty in accepting this as part of his destiny.

The gospels only contain a selection of the miracles that Jesus did, but the selection shows that he helped anyone in need without question, provided only that they showed faith in him. By the time this miracle was recorded in the gospels a generation after the death of Jesus, Christians were being widely rejected by the Jewish authorities and rejected in the synagogues.

It was important for the early Christians to realise that they must be open to all people just as Jesus had been, even if they seemed to be their enemies. This account of the raising of a synagogue president's daughter would help the first Christians – Jews for the most part – to come to terms with the consequences of their new faith.

Lazarus (Jn 11:1-44)

The raising of Lazarus, which is only recorded in John's Gospel, is by far the most dramatic and decisive of the miracles in which Jesus brought a dead person to life again. By the time Jesus reached Bethany, just outside Jerusalem, Lazarus had been dead and in a sealed tomb for four days. Under contemporary Jewish beliefs, the spirit would have left the body and the vicinity by then. Lazarus was truly dead.

Lazarus was the brother of Mary and Martha, who figure earlier in the gospels; Luke records that Jesus and the disciples visited their house during his journey from Galilee to Jerusalem (Lk 10:38-42). John says it was the same Mary who later anointed Jesus' feet with expensive, perfumed oil and wiped them with her hair shortly before he entered Jerusalem for the last time.

When the news that Lazarus was ill reached Jesus he was working beyond the River Jordan near the place where John the Baptist had baptised him. A short time before this he had visited Jerusalem for the Feast of Dedication, which falls in mid-December by modern reckoning, and had narrowly escaped stoning and arrest for blasphemy. Trans-Jordan was in a different administrative region from Jerusalem and Jesus may have gone there for safety.

When Jesus was told of his friend's illness he replied cryptically that it was not 'unto death' but 'for the glory of

God, so that the Son of God may be glorified by means of it' (Jn 11:4), and he delayed moving for two more days. He may well have thought that Lazarus was not going to die, or he may have meant that Lazarus' death would be the occasion for Jesus to reveal the full extent of his powers as Son of God. The reference to 'glory' echoes the miracle at Cana when Jesus turned water to wine and 'manifested his glory' (Jn 2:11).

Jesus told the disciples that he was returning to Judea, the region which contained Bethany and Jerusalem, and they protested to him that he would be placing himself in danger again. Jesus replied that there are twelve hours of daylight when you can see to walk, and twelve hours of darkness when you stumble. Jesus, 'the light of this world' (Jn 11:9) thought it was still safe for him to walk even in the dangerous vicinity of Jerusalem; his hours of darkness had not yet arrived.

Then Jesus told the disciples that Lazarus had fallen asleep but he was going to awaken him. The disciples thought Jesus meant the sleep of recovery from sickness. Jesus then told them plainly that Lazarus had died and that he was glad for their sake that he had not been there, 'so that you may believe' he added, implying that what he was about to do for Lazarus would deepen their faith. One of the disciples, Thomas, spoke to the others in words of moving devotion to Jesus: 'Let us also go, that we may die with him' (Jn 11:16).

Martha went a little way from the village to meet Jesus when she heard he was coming, while Mary stayed in the house with the many mourners who had come to console them. Consequently, Jesus and Martha had time to talk without a crowd surrounding them. In the course of their brief but intense conversation Jesus revealed the full extent and significance of what he was about to do, and Martha expressed her belief that he was indeed the expected Messiah.

As they met, Martha greeted Jesus: 'Lord, if you had been here my brother would not have died. And even now I know that whatever you ask from God, God will give you.'

'Your brother will rise again', replied Jesus.

'I know that he will rise again in the resurrection at the last day', said Martha.

'I am the resurrection and the life', Jesus replied. 'He who believes in me, though he die, yet shall he live, and whoever lives and believes in me shall never die. Do you believe this?'

'Yes, Lord' said Martha; 'I believe that you are the Christ, the Son of God, he who is coming into the world' (Jn 11:21-27).

Martha went to fetch Mary, who came, followed by mourners, to where Jesus and the disciples were waiting. She fell weeping at his feet and, like Martha, told him that if he had been there her brother would not have died. Jesus asked where they had buried him and they all invited Jesus to go and see. Jesus wept, the crowd exclaimed at his love for Lazarus, and some who knew of his reputation said that he could have kept Lazarus from dying.

When they arrived at the tomb carved out of the rock, Jesus told them to take away the stone which sealed its entrance. Martha objected that Lazarus had been dead for four days and his body would already be decomposing. Jesus reminded her of their recent conversation when she met him as he arrived, so the stone was removed as Jesus had ordered.

After lifting up his eyes and praying, Jesus cried out for Lazarus to come out of the tomb, and the dead man came out still wrapped around in the burial cloths. Jesus ordered him to be unbound and released.

The crowd was divided in its reactions. Some were led to believe in Jesus; others reported to the Pharisees what Jesus had just done. The Pharisees and temple priests immediately called an emergency meeting of the council, just as they had in the previous autumn after the Feast of Tabernacles when they had tried to arrest Jesus as he taught in the temple.

On that occasion Nicodemus had persuaded his council colleagues not to take any action against Jesus. This time there was more than blasphemous teaching involved, and they chose to interpret Jesus' actions as a threat to national security: 'If we let him go on thus, every one will believe in him, and the Romans will come and destroy both our holy place (the temple) and our nation' (Jn 11:48).

Their fears were quite reasonable ones. There had been many popular risings led by militant nationalists who had claimed to be messiahs, and the Romans were ruthless in suppressing anything which threatened their authority. If John's Gospel was finally edited late in the first century, as many think, it recorded all this after the Jewish-Roman war of 66-70 AD, which culminated in the destruction of Jerusalem and the temple.

Caiaphas, that year's Jewish high priest who as president of the Great Council would conduct Jesus' trial, told the meeting that it was better for one man to die for the people rather than the whole nation be destroyed (Jn 11:50). John's Gospel says that the remark was prophetic, because in another sense Jesus would indeed die not only for the Jewish nation, 'but to gather into one the children of God who are scattered abroad' (Jn 11:52).

Jesus and the disciples withdrew again from the area around Jerusalem, this time to a town some fifteen miles north in what had once been Samaria, where there was little sympathy for Jerusalem and its Jewish authorities. Meanwhile, the religious leaders began to discuss seriously how they could have Jesus executed, and they issued a general order for his arrest.

There is an obvious connection between the raising of Lazarus after burial and the resurrection of Jesus himself, but John's Gospel also links it in with Jesus' triumphal entry into Jerusalem displaying the traditional symbols of the Messiah. The connecting link is a supper at Bethany with Lazarus, Martha and Mary, the day before the triumphal entry. Mary anointed Jesus' feet with costly ointment. When Judas protested at the waste, he was told by Jesus that Mary was anticipating his burial. Jesus would be dead within the week.

The raising to life again of Lazarus is the seventh of the 'signs' in John's Gospel, chosen from the many other signs that John says Jesus did in the presence of his disciples, and recorded 'that you may believe that Jesus is the Christ, the Son of God, and that believing you may have life in his name' (Jn 20:31). After the raising of Lazarus in John's Gospel, as we have seen, comes the final week of Jesus' life which culminate in his death and resurrection.

Each of the signs reveals something of who Jesus really is and what he achieved, but the special significance of this seventh sign may be found in Jesus' assertion that he himself is the resurrection and the life of all who believe in him. That claim lies at the very heart of Christian belief. His own death and resurrection would be valueless if it could not be shared, but Jesus made it clear that it opened the way for all to share in his eternal life as Son of God.

The significance of the resurrection miracles

All the miracles were chosen by the author-editors of the gospels for the light they helped to throw on the crucifixion and resurrection of Jesus, and the consequences for the first Christians. As Jesus himself died and rose again, it might be thought that these particular miracles were even more significant than the others, but this assumption could be misleading.

Contrary to modern popular belief, the New Testament is emphatic that it was God who raised Jesus from the dead, rather than Jesus who raised himself. As in the other miracles, Jesus used the power of God to bring people back to life again, not any separate and distinct powers he might have of his own; there is no question of him acting independently of his Father as if he were another God.

The first Christians of the New Testament period believed that they shared fully in the risen life of Jesus, and so in full union with God himself, both before and after their own deaths. Their union with the risen Christ was closely connected with their baptism, they believed, as Paul reminds them:

'...all of us who have been baptised into Christ Jesus are baptised into his death. We were buried therefore with him by baptism into death, so that as Christ was raised from the dead by the glory of the Father, we too might walk in newness of life' (Rom 6:3-4).

Jesus had passed through death to a new kind of life where death had no power and held no fears for him. This is what he shared with all who believed in him.

Looking back on the resurrection miracles with these beliefs, they demonstrate that no human need is so desperate that it cannot be reached and remedied by God, not even death itself. Jesus raised the son of the widow of Nain because the dead man was her only son and she was in danger of being left destitute. Jesus' compassion was directed towards the mother as much as to her son, and it was her needs that Jesus most obviously met. The raising of Jairus' daughter demonstrates that the healing power of God's love expressed through Jesus can even reach beyond death.

Before the raising of Lazarus, Jesus told Martha that he himself was the resurrection and the life, and that all who believed in him would live after death and never die. Knowing that Lazarus was dead, Jesus waited long enough for it to be clear to everyone present that this was truly the raising of someone from the full finality of death. That also would be an important point for early Christian belief.

As Paul's letters to the Thessalonians indicate, the first Christians, like Christians now, needed such an unmistakable example of Christ's power beyond death as the raising of Lazarus. The Christians of Thessalonica, who were expecting the imminent return of Jesus in the Second Coming, had to be reassured by Paul that those who had already died would not be deprived of their share in Christ's triumph (1 Thess 4:13-18). As with Lazarus, Christians who have already died are as much within reach of the power of Christ as those who are alive. By his death and resurrection, Jesus broke through the barrier of death for all to follow him.

5

Healing blind people

Miracle	Matthew	Mark	Luke	John
Two blind men	9:27-31			
A blind man at Bethsaida		8:22-26		
A blind man born blind				9:1-7
Blind Bartimaeus	20:29-34	10:46-52	18:35-43	

Miracles of healed faculties

Nearly half of the miracles reported in the gospels are miracles of healing without any mention of demonic possession. This is by no means a hard-and-fast distinction, within the beliefs of the times, and the lack of any mention of demons may only mean that the accounts of these miracles are concentrating on other aspects of the cures.

In various ways, faith in Jesus was an important factor in most of them. Sometimes it was the faith of the person in need of healing, but on several occasions Jesus called on the faith of friends or relatives. On one notable occasion it was the faith of a non-Jew, the Roman centurion whose servant was lying back at his house paralysed; Jesus told the centurion that his faith was greater than that of anyone he had found amongst Jesus own people, the descendants of Abraham.

Of these miraculous healings, nine refer to the cure of impaired faculties: sight, hearing, speech, hands and limbs, and these are the ones which will be examined in this and the next chapter. They seem to play a particularly important part in the gospels' build-up to the crucifixion and resurrection of Jesus. This would be one of the reasons why they were selected by the apostles as they taught their people about the significance of the saving work of Jesus, and its practical consequences for their lives.

As the gospels themselves do not follow any one chronological sequence of events when portraying the ministry of Jesus, there is no real point in trying to look at these miracles in order of their occurrence. The best we can say is that Jesus performed some of them in Galilee earlier in his ministry, some in Jerusalem during various visits he made, and one of them while he was being arrested the night before his execution.

Two blind men (Mt 9:27-31)

In one of the simplest descriptions of a miracle, Matthew's Gospel records that Jesus was met by two blind men as he was leaving Capernaum. This is one of a collection of ten miracles in this and the preceding chapter of this gospel which cover a wide range of needs met by Jesus, from leprosy to paralysis, from demonic possession to blindness.

Two blind men followed him along the road calling out for him to have mercy on them and addressing him as 'Son of David', one of the traditional titles of the Messiah. At first Jesus seems to have ignored them, but they followed him into the house, presumably the house in Capernaum where he had established the base for his ministry in Galilee.

Jesus turned to the two men and said, 'Do you believe that I am able to do this?' They assured him that they did. Jesus then touched their eyes and said, 'According to your faith be it done to you' (Mt 9:28-29), and they found that they could see.

Jesus told them sternly not to let anyone know what he had done for them, but naturally they spread his fame through all the district. The title 'Son of David' with which the two men had addressed Jesus indicates why he told them to keep silent about the manner of their healing, and why he would not do anything for them in the open street.

King David had liberated the Hebrew nation a thousand years earlier and conquered the neighbouring peoples. Many Jews expected the coming Messiah to be another David – hence the title – and free Palestine from the Roman occupation. In view of such crudely nationalist beliefs about the Messiah, Jesus could not afford to be widely acclaimed as Messiah at this stage in his ministry. He must first try to get people to understand what kind of Messiah he was.

A blind man at Bethsaida (Mk 8:22-26)

Bethsaida was a new town in the time of Jesus, built by the Jewish ruler of the region, Philip the Tetrarch, on the eastern banks of the River Jordan at the northern end of the Sea of Galilee, and not very far from Capernaum.

A blind man from somewhere outside Bethsaida was brought to Jesus by people who begged him to heal the man by touching him. Jesus first took the man by the hand and led him out of the town, no doubt again to try to avoid any publicity for what he was about to do.

Once outside the town, Jesus spat on the man's eyes and laid his hands on them, then he asked him if he could see anything. The man looked up and said he could see men, but they looked like trees, walking.

Jesus laid his hands on the man's eyes again, and this time the man looked around intently and found that he could see everything clearly. Jesus sent him back home again and told him not to pass through Bethsaida on the way. Again, Jesus was trying to keep the miracle quiet for fear of becoming the centre of the wrong kind of messianic expectations.

The gospels are based on various versions of the apostolic tradition. Mark's Gospel is the only one to record this particular miracle, and it is clear that it was selected and placed where it is in the structure of Mark's Gospel as a comment on what immediately follows.

In Mark's Gospel Jesus and his disciples are next found further north, in the villages around Caesarea Philippi at the foot of Mount Hermon. There Jesus began to question his disciples' beliefs in an exchange which turned out to be one of the great turning points of the gospel story.

He first asked the disciples what people were saying about him. Who did they think he was? The disciples replied that some thought he was John the Baptist, who by this time had been executed by Herod Antipas. Others were saying that he was Elijah, the Hebrew prophet of nine centuries earlier who was expected to appear again as the herald of the Messiah. Others still were saying that Jesus was the latest in the long line of Hebrew prophets.

Jesus then asked the disciples what they themselves thought. Peter replied that Jesus was the 'Christ' – the Greek word for the Hebrew 'Messiah'.

At this point Matthew's Gospel inserts the passage about Peter as the rock on which Jesus will build his Church, but Mark goes straight on with the first of the three instances when Jesus told the disciples just what kind of Messiah he was:

'And he began to teach them that the Son of man must suffer many things, and be rejected by the elders and the chief priests and the scribes, and be killed, and after three days rise again. And he said this plainly' (Mk 8:31-32).

Peter began to remonstrate with Jesus, and Jesus rebuked him sharply as 'Satan', 'For you are not on the side of God, but of men' (Mk 8:33). Jesus immediately called all who were present, close disciples and crowd, to come near to him, then he told them that if anyone wanted to follow him he must also be prepared to accept sufferings as appalling as crucifixion.

Twice more on their way to Jerusalem Jesus would repeat to his disciples his warning of what awaited him when they reached the city (Mk 9:30-32; 10:32-34). At each warning the disciples were reduced to silence or responded in ways which showed that they did not understand the implications of what Jesus was telling them. Their reactions were hardly surprising, for everyone in those times was familiar with the horrors of execution by crucifixion. It was inconceivable to them that Jesus would deliberately journey towards such an end, particularly if he was the Messiah.

When Jesus restored the sight of the blind man brought to him at Bethsaida, Jesus had to touch him more than once before he saw everything clearly. So too with the disciples. Even after they had acknowledged that Jesus was the Messiah, they needed repeated explanations before they began to see what Jesus himself meant by Messiah, and how he intended to complete his messianic mission.

A blind man born blind (Jn 9:1-7)

The only record in John's Gospel of Jesus healing a blind man is set in Jerusalem, near the temple during the Feast of Tabernacles. This great harvest festival was held in the autumn at the end of the agricultural year; the people built temporary shelters – tabernacles – in the fields for this harvest, to gather the last of their crops before the winter rains started. It was one of the three pilgrimage feasts, and the Temple area of Jerusalem would be crowded.

The man had been blind from birth and was begging by the side of the road. As so often happened with the miracles, an accidental encounter with Jesus led to his healing. Jesus' disciples noticed him as they passed and, reflecting the normal belief that afflictions were caused by sins, they asked Jesus whether the man himself had sinned or his parents. Jesus replied that neither he nor his parents had sinned, but that his blindness was an opportunity for God's power to be revealed. Jesus added that as long as he was in the world he was the light of the world.

Jesus spat on the ground to make a little clay and rubbed

it onto the man's eyes. Then he told him to wash his eyes in the pool of Siloam, one of the largest of the open storage cisterns for Jerusalem's water supply. It was at the other end of the old city from the Temple, and by the time the man returned from washing, able to see for the first time in his life, Jesus had disappeared into the crowds.

The restoration of sight to the familiar figure started arguments amongst those who were used to seeing him begging. Some said it was the same man who had been blind from birth; others said it was someone else. When they asked him what had happened, the man told them that it was Jesus who had healed him, and how he had done it.

At this point another factor enters into the story. The man was taken to the Pharisees to explain what had happened, and as the man was describing the incident it emerged that Jesus had healed him on a sabbath day. This started an argument amongst the religious leaders. They did not doubt that Jesus had healed the man, but some of the Pharisees said that if Jesus had broken the religious laws by healing on the sabbath his powers could not come from God. Jesus must be a sinner if he broke the law so blatantly. Others argued that Jesus could not be a sinner if he had power to perform miracles such as this. The man was called back and asked what he thought about Jesus. Cautiously, he just replied that Jesus was a prophet.

The Pharisees were reluctant to accept that the stories circulating about Jesus might be true, so they refused to believe that the man really had been born blind or that he was the same man. They next questioned the man's parents, who confirmed that this was indeed their son and that he had been born blind; beyond that they would not go. The religious authorities had already ruled that anyone who said that Jesus was the Messiah would be excluded from their local synagogue. That would be the end of any normal life or prosperity for them. The man's parents therefore told the Pharisees that their son was old enough to speak for himself; they should ask him.

So the Pharisees again turned to the man and asked him

to agree with them, under oath, that Jesus was a sinner. But the man would not be drawn into that kind of argument; he would only say that he knew he had been blind and he knew that he could now see. They asked him to describe the event again. The man began to lose his patience. He retorted that he had already told them and added, 'Why do you want to hear it again? Do you too want to become his disciples?' (Jn 9:27). They pressed him further, only looking for some way of discrediting Jesus, until the man rounded on them: 'Never since the world began has it been heard that any one opened the eyes of a man born blind. If this man were not from God, he could do nothing' (Jn 9:32-33). Angrily, they dismissed him.

Jesus heard what had happened, so he looked for the man and revealed who he was. The man told Jesus that he believed him, and he worshipped him. Jesus told him that he had come into the world to deliver the judgement that it is the blind who can really see, and those with sight who are blind. Touchingly, some Pharisees asked Jesus if they too were blind. If they were blind, replied Jesus, they would be without guilt, but if they thought they could see they remained unforgiven.

John's Gospel emphasises the significance of this miracle by placing it between two accounts of confrontations between Jesus and the religious leaders. In the first one, with the Pharisees in the temple area, Jesus had told them that he was the light of the world, and he had so enraged them that they tried to stone him.

Lights played an important role in the celebration of the Feast of Tabernacles, when that confrontation took place. A great candelabrum was lit in one of the temple courtyards, and every home had lamps burning throughout the feast. They symbolised the prosperity given by God and the light shed by the law God had revealed through Moses.

In these surroundings, Jesus claimed that he was the light of the world. To his audience, it was an unmistakable assertion that he thought he was God, and the Pharisees naturally challenged him; but he had the sympathy of the crowd and for the time being the authorities could do nothing to stop him.

But Jesus went straight on to challenge the ordinary Jews as well, who thought that mere descent from Abraham guaranteed them the privileges of God's promises. Abraham was the first Hebrew to receive a covenant from God, and all Jews traced their descent from him.

In a cryptic remark, Jesus told his audience that Abraham had been glad to see his day. Mockingly, they riposted that Jesus was not yet fifty; how could he have seen Abraham? Jesus replied that he was already alive before Abraham was born. At this the crowd lost its patience and took up stones to stone him. Jesus hurriedly left.

After the miracle and the harsh treatment of the healed man by the religious leaders, Jesus pointedly claimed that he was the true shepherd, the good shepherd who was prepared to give his life for his sheep. The others who claimed to be shepherds, Jesus said, were thieves and robbers who deserted the sheep when they needed help and protection.

Such claims made by Jesus in Jerusalem itself could not be long ignored by the religious authorities, and eventually such teaching would cost Jesus his life. But at present many of the people believed that his miracles lent credibility to his claims, and the authorities did not think the time had yet come when they could safely stop him.

Blind Bartimaeus (Mt 29:29-34; Mk 10:46-52; Lk 18:35-43)

The first three of the four gospels make Jericho, at the southern end of the River Jordan's deep valley, the final stop for Jesus on his way to Jerusalem for the climax of his life and ministry. According to the other gospel, John's, Jesus had been near Jerusalem shortly before and had raised Lazarus from the dead. This had so alarmed the religious authorities that the high priest, Caiaphas, had advised the Great Council that Jesus was a threat to national security and it would be best for all if he died. Jesus had tactfully withdrawn from the area.

As the greatest of the three pilgrimage festivals approached, the combined feast of Passover and Unleavened Bread, Jesus decided that he must confront the authorities with his claims and force them to accept or reject him once and for all. He and the disciples took the road to Jerusalem again and crossed the Jordan Valley just north of the Dead Sea. As they were passing through Jericho a blind beggar called Bartimaeus shouted out and hailed Jesus as Son of David.

Those around tried to quieten him, but Bartimaeus only shouted the messianic title more loudly, together with a plea for pity. Jesus stopped and told the people around to bring Bartimaeus to him, so the blind man threw off his cloak and went to him. Jesus asked him what he wanted him to do for him. Addressing Jesus formally as 'my master', Bartimaeus asked him to let him see again. Jesus told him to go, for his faith had saved him. His sight returned immediately, and he followed Jesus along the road.

There was to be a further incident in Jericho before Jesus began the long climb up the road to Jerusalem. A short tax collector named Zacchaeus darted about in the crowd trying glimpse the famous teacher. In the end he climbed into a tree, where Jesus saw him and called to him to come down because he wished to lodge in his house.

Zacchaeus practised a notoriously corrupt profession, and Jesus was again criticised for befriending such a person. But Zacchaeus volunteered to give half of his wealth to the poor and to restore four times the amount of any tax money he had taken unjustly. Jesus told him that salvation had come to his house that day, and that the Son of man came to search out and save what was lost.

Taken together, the two incidents illustrate the gospel themes of Jesus' special mission to the deprived and rejected members of society, the new sight which can only come from God, and Jesus' call for those who acknowledge him as Messiah to follow him. Jesus emphasised the point with the parable of the talents, the symbols of gifts from God. They must be used responsibly, he implied, and not hoarded, or God would take them back again.

For the first Christians, the miracle for Bartimaeus, the call of Zacchaeus and the parable of the talents would all point to the utter condemnation of the Jewish authorities as Jesus went to his death at their hands.

The significance of the miracles of sight

The four miracles in which Jesus gave sight to blind people are accompanied in the gospels by unusually detailed indications of their deeper significance. The opening chapter of John's Gospel, modelled on the opening chapter of the Book of Genesis, asserts that Jesus was the light of God, shining in the darkness, which the darkness could not overcome. Just as the darkness could not overwhelm the light decreed by God at the creation of the world, so too no evil could overwhelm Jesus.

But Jesus was also 'the true light that enlightens every man' (Jn 1:9), and the miracles of sight show him restoring that light to people who have lost it. No person who was literally blind could be unaware of their impediment and they would long to have sight. Unhappily, those who are spiritually blind might well think that they can see better than anyone, as Jesus pointed out to the Pharisees. In that case, he could do nothing to help them. Jesus could only help those who recognise their needs and show some kind of faith in him, either personally or through their friends.

All this is entirely consistent with the dynamics of love expressed by Jesus throughout the gospels. The divine initiative of love looks for response. Where people deny that Jesus is the embodiment of God's love, or deny that they need his help, he can only leave them to their blindness.

6

Miracles of
healing various faculties

Miracle	Matthew	Mark	Luke	John
The centurion's servant	8:5-13		7:1-10	
A paralysed man in Capernaum		2:1-12		
A man with a withered hand	12:9-14	3:1-6	6:6-11	
A paralysed man at the pool of Bethsaida				5:1-9
A deaf-mute		7:31-37		

Miracles where Jesus healed blind people have clear significance as signs of Jesus as the light of the world, so it has been appropriate to discuss them as a separate group in the previous chapter. Five other miracles show Jesus healing other impaired human faculties: paralysed limbs (twice), a hand, deafness and a speech defect.

As with the miracles to heal blindness, there is no mention of demonic possession in the accounts of these miracles, but again it would be a mistake to conclude from this that Jesus himself, his disciples and the Christians for whom the gospels were first written believed that no evil was involved. As in the case of the healing of the man born blind, reported in John's Gospel, the disciples of Jesus readily attributed any physical defect to sin. In that instance Jesus stated firmly that neither the man nor his parents had sinned, but it was a common assumption to make and there was a rigid dividing line drawn between personal sin and personal evil.

As with so many of the miracles, there is a strong emphasis on faith in some of the miracles in this group, but by no means all of them. Where faith is emphasised, it happens that the faith is shown by others, and the faith of the person actually in need of healing is not mentioned. That faith could be effective on behalf of others would be a very important point for the first Christians with their strong sense of community. It underlined that responsibility of members of the community for each other which figures in the New Testament letters.

The centurion's servant (Mt 8:5-13; Lk 7:1-10)

Matthew's Gospel is characterised by a number of discourses in which the teaching Jesus gave is collected together under various topics. The Sermon on the Mount (Mt 5-7) is one such discourse. It quotes the kind of teaching Jesus gave to his disciples and to the crowds about the new way of life he had come to offer them, and what would be expected of them if they accepted his invitation to follow him 'so that you may be sons of your Father who is in heaven' (Mt 5:45).

In many ways Jesus urged the crowd to abandon the deeply entrenched attitudes of their times, particularly about the law, justice and revenge. He seemed to be demanding impossible standards from them, but the discourse ends with the observation that 'the crowds were astonished at his teaching, for he taught them as one who had authority, and not as their scribes' (Mt 7:28-29).

It is unlikely that Jesus ever delivered this discourse just as Matthew's Gospel presents it, for much of the teaching of Jesus it contains is to be found scattered about the other gospels. But there can be no doubts about the authenticity of the teaching, nor about the impression of exceptional authority Jesus conveyed whenever he taught.

In Matthew's Gospel the Sermon on the Mount is followed immediately by two miracles, which helped to demonstrate to the crowds that Jesus' exceptional authority came from God. The first of the two miracles will receive more detailed attention in the next chapter. It occurred as Jesus was on his way back to Capernaum, by the Sea of Galilee. Waiting for Jesus on the road was a leper who simply told Jesus that he could heal him if he wished to. Jesus immediately did so.

The second miracle arose from a request by a Roman officer whose servant was ill. Although Galilee had a Jewish ruler appointed by the Romans, it was also part of the Roman province of Syria. As an important town in a turbulent area, Capernaum had a Roman garrison, part of the force of Roman soldiers stationed throughout Palestine. The Roman centurion in charge was no Jew, but he was clearly sympathetic towards the Jewish religion and may even have been a 'God-fearer", who attended Jewish worship without becoming a Jewish convert.

The centurion had paid for a Jewish synagogue to be built near his headquarters in Capernaum. When his servant fell ill, the centurion turned to Jesus, the local Jew with the reputation for healing, and waited for him at the main gate into the town. No doubt there was an audience, for the town gate was usually the main meeting place for news, gossip and the administration of justice by the town's elders.

However much he might have been respected, the centurion was still the local commander of a foreign army of occupation. Although the Jews themselves had originally called in the Romans to stop a civil war between Jewish factions, that had long since been forgotten by Jewish extremists. Groups such as the zealots hated presence of the Roman troops as a blasphemous defilement of the holy land, and they opposed the payment of Roman taxes on the grounds that the only king Jews could recognise was God himself.

As Jesus entered Capernaum, the centurion approached him and told him simply that his servant was lying paralysed at home and in terrible distress. Jesus immediately offered to come to the Roman officer's home to heal the servant, an act which would have probably involved breaking the strict Jewish religious laws. The soldier told Jesus that he did not feel worthy for Jesus to enter his house, and in any case there was no need for him to do so. Jesus only had to command it, said the soldier, and his servant would be healed.

He went on to explain why he believed this:

'For I am a man under authority, with soldiers under me; and I say to one, Go, and he goes, and to another, Come, and he comes, and to my slave, Do this, and he does it' (Mt 8:9).

The Roman officer was saying that he had power of command, but his power was not his own. It came from the supreme power of the Roman emperor, delegated to him as the local commanding officer. The emperor's power was channelled into Galilee through this Roman soldier. The centurion recognised the same kind of authority in Jesus, absolute power delegated to him by God. He told Jesus that he did not expect him to come to his Gentile house; if Jesus merely gave the order, the servant would be healed. Whatever was harming him, the soldier implied, would be helpless before the supreme power delegated to Jesus.

Surprised by the soldier's insight, Jesus used words which must have shocked his disciples and any other Jews present:

'Truly, I say to you, not even in Israel have I found such faith. I tell you, many will come from east and west and sit at table with Abraham, Isaac and Jacob in the kingdom of heaven, while the sons of the kingdom will be thrown into outer darkness; there men will weep and gnash their teeth' (Mt 8:10-12).

Jesus told the centurion to go, and he commanded that it be done for him as he had believed. He found that his servant was healed.

By the time the final version of Matthew's Gospel came to be written, Christianity had indeed spread far to the east and west, many non-Jews had become Christians and Jerusalem had been destroyed at the climax of the Jewish-Roman War. Jesus' words to the Roman centurion would already be seen as specially significant. Perhaps, also, the centurion's reference to being 'under' authority himself helped reconcile the first Christians to the Roman execution of Jesus. The soldiers who carried out the crucifixion were obeying orders, even if they were the unjust orders of a weak Roman magistrate.

A paralysed man in Capernaum (Mt 9:1-8; Mk 2:1-12; Lk 5:17-26)

The gospels set this miracle early in Jesus' Galilean ministry, when he had already begun to attract large crowds and the unwelcome attention of the official religious authorities. More than once already, Jesus had crossed by boat to another shore of the Sea of Galilee or had tried unsuccessfully to get away unnoticed to a quiet place, to escape from the crowds and find time for prayer.

On this occasion Jesus was in a house in Capernaum, possibly Peter's house or the one used as his base, and the house and its doorway were crowded with people listening to Jesus teach. Four men arrived carrying a paralysed friend on a stretcher but found that they could not get near Jesus. So keen were they to get their friend near Jesus that they took him and his stretcher on to the flat roof of the house, which would be reached by an outside stair. Then they pulled away part of the roof and let their friend down on ropes in front of Jesus.

The man's paralysis was obvious but Jesus saw a deeper need than physical healing. Moved by the faith of the friends who had gone to such trouble, Jesus looked down at the paralysed man and told him that his sins were forgiven.

There were scribes present, skilled professional writers

and administrators whose main work was producing accurate copies of the scrolls of the Hebrew law and other sacred scriptures. They were highly respected and considered to be experts in the works they copied. Whatever effect Jesus words had on the paralytic and his friends, the scribes reacted angrily.

Hebrew religious teaching made it clear that only God could forgive sins, and the scribes were offended because Jesus had spoken as if he himself had authority to forgive. They interpreted Jesus' words as a blasphemous claim to divinity.

Jesus realised what the scribes were thinking and he challenged them in the presence of the crowd. 'Which is easier,' he asked them, 'to say to the paralytic, Your sins are forgiven, or to say, Rise, take up your pallet and walk?' (Mk 2:9). Then he told them that he would show them that the Son of man had authority on earth to forgive sins, and he turned to the paralytic and said, 'I say to you, rise, take up your pallet and go home' (Mk 2:11). The man got up, picked up the stretcher on which he had been lying and walked out in the sight of everyone present. The miracle created a sensation, with everyone praising God and saying that they had never seen anything like it.

'Son of man' may seem a weak title for Jesus to claim in this and other passages in the gospels, but at his trial Jesus indicated that when he used this title he was thinking of the great apocalyptic prophecies in Daniel 7. There the 'Son of man' is the messianic king, sent by God in the world's final age to rule over all peoples and establish the eternal kingdom of God (Dan 7:13-27). With this precedent from Hebrew religious tradition defining its meaning, it was an even more powerful title than 'Son of God'.

In this incident, the visible miracle is a sign pointing to the deeper miracle; the cure of the man's paralysis indicated that Jesus had removed the man's sins. This would be of the utmost importance for the beliefs of the first Christians, because they believed that sin could do them far more harm than any physical disability. They must look to Jesus for the forgiveness of their sins rather than for physical benefits, because their sins were a fundamental impediment to their relationship with God.

In Mark's Gospel this miracle is the first in a series of five incidents where Jesus encounters different kinds of questioning or condemnation of his actions. At the end of the fifth of these incidents, the cure of the man with a withered hand, there is the first mention of plans to kill Jesus. Just as the scribes in the house in Capernaum interpreted Jesus' words of forgiveness as blasphemy, so too the charge which eventually condemned Jesus in the highest Jewish court was also one of blasphemy. The account of this miracle points forward to the decisive events of the last days of Jesus' life.

A man with a withered hand (Mt 12:9-14; Mk 3:1-6; Lk 6:6-11)

On a later occasion Jesus caused far deeper anger amongst his growing ranks of religious opponents by healing a man with a withered hand on a sabbath day. The act in itself would not have been offensive, for there is no mention of Jesus forgiving the man's sins. But scribes and Pharisees present interpreted it as a deliberate breach of the sabbath laws, and Jesus encouraged them to see it as such.

Each of the first three gospels places the incident immediately after a skirmish with the Pharisees when they saw Jesus and his disciples plucking ears of corn as they passed through a field, rubbing out the grain and munching it. It was a sabbath, and the Pharisees seized the opportunity of accusing them all of sabbath-breaking.

Jesus sharply reminded the Pharisees of a famous incident in which King David had broken equally important laws by taking the sacred sacrificial loaves from the sanctuary and eating them when he was on the run from Saul. He added that the temple priests work on the sabbath without guilt, and that he was greater than the temple. In any case, Jesus said, 'The sabbath was made for man, not man for the sabbath;' and using the powerful messianic title again, Jesus added, 'so the Son of man is lord even of the sabbath' (Mk 3:27).

They were provocative words, which to the Pharisees could only mean that Jesus was claiming personal authority greater than the religious laws revealed by God to Moses. The group of Pharisees followed Jesus when he and the disciples went on their way and into a synagogue.

Amongst the congregation in the synagogue was a man with a withered hand, and the Pharisees watched to see if Jesus would do anything for him. Jesus called the man to him, then challenged his critics, 'Is it lawful on the sabbath to do good or to do harm, to save life or to kill?' (Mk 3:4).

They remained silent while Jesus looked around at them with anger. Then he told the man to stretch out his hand, and as he did so the hand was made whole again. The Pharisees left the synagogue and immediately conferred with Herodians about the best way of destroying Jesus. As supporters of the local Jewish ruler appointed by the Romans, the Herodians were usually hated by the Pharisees. That the two groups could plot together is a measure of the anger and concern Jesus was arousing amongst members of powerful Jewish political and religious factions. Their reasons for hating him differed radically, but they were prepared to sink their differences to be rid of him.

Jesus' attitude towards the sabbath seems to have made devout Jewish groups particularly angry, but strict Christian groups can still be made as angry by what they consider to be violations of Sunday. The sabbath was the day of rest ordered by Hebrew law for the last day of each week, to commemorate the creation of the world, which God completed in six days and then rested, and the escape from Egypt, when God saved the Israelites from unremitting labour.

Taken literally, the religious laws required every person and every domestic animal to cease work for twenty-four hours from sunset on Friday. Like all Hebrew laws, the basic sabbath law was believed to have been dictated by God to

Moses. The detailed applications were evolved later, often by enlightened and realistic lawyers recording the decisions of local courts, as the nation's way of life changed.

Problems arose when religious groups took the law literally as the revelation of God, and applied its details uncompromisingly without any regard for its original spirit. Jesus cut through the letter of the sabbath laws to the underlying principle and behaved accordingly. People who believed that every detail of the written law was the revealed will of God thought Jesus was blaspheming.

Once more, this miracle points forward to the last days of Jesus and helps to throw light on what was really happening during them. Condemned for blasphemy against God, Jesus was raised by God from the dead and vindicated. His resurrection was also a condemnation of religious legalism, and the clearest possible proof to Christians that Jesus had freed them from it. They could not be saved by law, nor condemned by it.

As Paul put it, Jesus had set aside all legal obligations by nailing them to his cross. No one could now condemn them for breaking them. They were now ruled by the principle of love, which transcends law and binds everything together in perfect harmony (Col 2:8-3:14).

A paralysed man at the pool of Bethesda (Jn 5:1-9)

John's Gospel, which is the only one to record this miracle, says that it occurred at a pool fed by springs just north of Jerusalem's temple area. Jesus had gone to the city again for one of the main religious festivals; the gospel does not say which one. The pool's main purpose was to provide water for the temple's needs, but the people believed that the water would cure the first person to step into it whenever the springs made the water move. It was surrounded by paving, and five porches gave access to the steps leading into the water. Among the crowd waiting for the pool to move lay a paralysed man who had no one to help him into the water.

Consequently, he had no chance of being first, and so of being cured. Jesus was moved as much by his frustration as by his illness, and simply told him to get up, take his bedding and walk. The man did so and Jesus moved away before the crowd could notice what had happened.

The cured man was immediately accused of breaking the law. It was a sabbath day when Jewish law forbade all work, and he was caught carrying bedding, right by the temple area itself where the law would be most strictly enforced. The man told his accusers what had happened, but Jesus had gone, so he could not tell his accusers who it was that had healed him.

Later in the day, Jesus came across the man again in one of the temple courtyards and he took the opportunity to link the cure with a more profound, spiritual healing. He told the man that he had been made whole, and should no more sin. Perhaps to clear himself, the man went back to the Jewish authorities and told them that it was Jesus who had healed him. They turned their anger on Jesus, who was already seen as a threat to religious tradition and the laws which guarded it. His reply demonstrated how well grounded their fears were.

Charged with sabbath-breaking, Jesus replied by claiming the same powers and privileges as God himself: 'My Father is working still, and I am working' (Jn 5:17). The blasphemy was clear enough, but Jesus extended his explanation so that every Jew present would recognise what he was claiming. As the Son, he said, he was working under the direct commands of his Father, God, and could do whatever God could do. Like God his Father, who 'raises the dead and gives them life, so also the Son gives life to whom he will' (Jn 5:21).

Jesus went on to use titles which in Jewish religious tradition could only apply to the Messiah himself. The time had already come, he said, when the dead would hear the voice of the Son of God, and would live as a consequence. Furthermore, Jesus claimed that he had supreme judicial authority as Son of man. Jesus again used the title which would bring the death sentence down on him when the authorities finally arrested him and brought him to trial.

Hammering home his claims, Jesus told his audience that when they had asked John the Baptist about him, John had told them the truth; but Jesus said that his own miracles were an even greater witness than John's testimony. If they refused to accept him after that kind of evidence it could only mean that they lacked God's love, he concluded, whatever Jewish history might say, and Moses himself would condemn them.

John's Gospel says that the Jews had tried to kill Jesus earlier in the confrontation, but his authoritative and detailed assertion of the real power behind his actions seems to have silenced them. He was able to leave for Galilee unhindered.

A deaf-mute (Mk 7:31-37)

By this stage of his ministry Jesus' main concern was to instruct his disciples, but he was increasingly hindered by the crowds which sought him out wherever he went. One such crowd containing many sick people followed him into the hills above the Sea of Galilee, where a deaf-mute was brought to him. Jesus took him to one side away from the crowd. Then he healed him by putting his fingers into his ears and spittle on his tongue, accompanied by a command in the local Aramaic dialect, 'Be opened!' (Mk 7:34).

Once again, Jesus told the man and his friends to keep quiet about the cure, but they told everyone. Others in need pressed forward and were healed, and the crowd was overwhelmed by the wonder of it all. There were real dangers in this kind of adulation, particularly as Northern Galilee was notorious for its armed resistance movements.

At this stage of his plans it was essential for Jesus to avoid the crisis of an armed messianic rising. The crowd could easily think he was the invincible 'Son of David", the messianic hero God would send to liberate them. That would be fatal if they then expected him to lead an armed rebellion against the Roman occupation.

As with the faculty of sight, other main human faculties can be used symbolically as well as literally. Then as now, sight is a symbol of the rational ability to understand and to reason, as well as the physical ability to see things. Used as an idiom, impaired sight refers to defective understanding, as in 'Can you not see what I mean?' and 'I cannot see any solution to the problem.' It occurs in proverbs for deliberate refusal to understand, such as 'None so blind as those that will not see!'

Similarly, limbs, hands, ears and tongue are all used idiomatically of human mental abilities and attitudes, as well as in their literal sense of physical abilities. We speak of 'strong-arm' men for domineering people, and long-legged is an idiom for speed. People are 'handy' if they are willing to help; they 'lend an ear' to us when they show a desire to understand or be sympathetic. 'Tongue' is a normal synonym for language itself as well as for the various different languages, and it can symbolise the whole process of communication.

When Jesus cured various defective faculties in people, there is every reason to believe that they were literally able to see again, to walk, to use their hands, to hear and to speak. But such healings were also symbolic of his ability to restore defective human spiritual faculties as well. He could make it possible for people to respond effectively to God, and to communicate effectively with each other. It became possible for them to forgive as they themselves had been forgiven, and they could overcome the difficulties of expressing the values of Jesus in their everyday lives.

The crucifixion and bodily resurrection of Jesus are powerful symbols of the restoration and perfection of human faculties by God. Jesus' human faculties were literally destroyed at the crucifixion, by the nailing of his hands and feet, and the slow disintegration of all his physical abilities. The gospels emphasise that his risen body was the same body that was crucified, as his wounds so clearly indicated, and Jesus used his risen body to communicate with his disciples and friends, just as he had done before his crucifixion. The healed human faculties of Jesus' risen body symbolised the healing of all who would be united to him and share his risen life. They too could relate to others by the same ideal standards as Jesus himself related to others, and by the same power.

As with the other miracles, these were selected from the many that Jesus did to help the first Christians to understand the full significance of the death and resurrection of Jesus, and what he made available to all who believed in him.

7

Other miracles
of healing

Miracle	Matthew	Mark	Luke	John
Peter's mother-in-law	8:14-15	1:29-31	4:38-39	
A leper	8:1-4	1:40-45	5:12-16	
A woman with an issue of blood	9:20-33	5:25-34	8:43-48	
The son of an official at Capernaum				4:46-54
A dropsical man			14:1-6	
Ten lepers			17:11-19	
The high priest's slave			22:50-51	

Although the remaining miracles of healing are not concerned with particular human physical faculties, three of them are about conditions which would make the person ritually impure under the Jewish religious laws. Two of these three deal with leprosy, a general term for skin diseases which entailed the unfortunate victims in exclusion from their families and communities because of the fear that their disease was contagious. In the case of the third, the unusual issue of blood rendered the woman ritually unclean under the laws detailed in the Book of Leviticus. By healing them, Jesus removed the cause of their exclusion and enabled them to become normal members of their communities again.

Two of the miracles, the healing of Peter's mother-in-law in Capernaum and of the official's son at Capernaum, are cures of unspecified fevers. The cure of the dropsical man emphasises the special place the poor have in God's love, by contrast with the special attention society pays to the rich and privileged. In healing the high priest's slave Jesus showed that he had time for compassionate healing even of his enemies at the very moment of his arrest and within hours of his own death. Faith again figures largely in some of these miracles.

Peter's mother-in-law (Mt 8:14-15; Mk 1:29-31; Lk 4:38-39)

The brief and simple description of this miracle, recorded in the first three gospels, occurred on a sabbath in Capernaum near the beginning of Jesus' ministry. He left the synagogue and went to the home of Simon Peter and Andrew, together with James and John, so he was accompanied by the four disciples he had so far invited to follow him. Simon told Jesus that his mother-in-law was lying in the house feverishly ill. Jesus went to her, took her by the hand and lifted her up; the fever immediately left her and she was even able to attend immediately to their needs.

Later in his ministry, when Jesus had aroused the strenuous opposition of the official Jewish religious parties, he would no doubt have been attacked for healing someone on the sabbath. But Jesus was still little known and this healing attracted no more opposition than the exorcism he had just performed in the synagogue. By the evening, however, the word had got round, and the whole town was gathered around the door of the house, bringing with them the sick and possessed for him to cure.

A leper (Mt 8:1-4; Mk 1:40-45; Lk 5:12-16)

Three gospels record this miracle (which received brief mention in the previous chapter of this book); but each of them places it in a slightly different position. These differences are a useful clue to the subtle way the gospel writers indicated the significance of the things Jesus did and said.

Mark's Gospel uses it as one of the incidents in a typical day of Jesus' early ministry, immediately after he had healed Simon Peter's mother-in-law. Luke's Gospel sets it immediately after Jesus had been teaching on a sabbath in Capernaum, by implication in the synagogue. But Matthew's Gospel presents it as the immediate sequel to the Sermon on the Mount, a miracle performed by Jesus as he was going down the hillside on the path back to Capernaum.

Matthew's is the most dramatic and pointed setting of the story. Jesus had so impressed his disciples and the other people who listened to him on the hillside that they had exclaimed that he spoke with an unusual authority, very different from the teaching they normally heard from their official religious teachers. On the way back to Capernaum Jesus was confronted by a leper, a description which could cover a number of skin diseases believed to be contagious: itches, swellings, eruptions or spots (Lev 14:54-56). Such people were excluded from normal communities and had to warn people to keep away from them.

The leper came to Jesus and knelt before him. It is not difficult to imagine the crowd and Jesus' disciples watching the scene closely. Then the leper simply said, 'Lord, if you will, you can make me clean.' Jesus touched him and replied, 'I will; be clean' (Mt 8:2-3). The leprosy left him immediately.

Hebrew law provided for people who were cured after being declared lepers. They were to show themselves to the local priest, the guardian of traditional knowledge, who would then examine them and certify whether they really were cured and could enter normal social life again. The cured person then offered specified sacrifices to God as a thanksgiving, and also as a public declaration of purity (Lev 14).

As he sent him on his way to the priest, Jesus ordered the man not to tell anyone how he had been cured. This frequent command by Jesus, that the people he healed should keep quiet, was to avoid mistaken popular expectations that Jesus would fulfil their political aspirations. Mark's and Luke's Gospels report that the man went about telling everyone what had happened, and Jesus had to withdraw from work in the towns. The crowds still sought him out, however, in the less inhabited places to which he now went.

The miracle is an example of simple faith, as well as of Jesus' compassion. In the setting Matthew's Gospel gives it, the cure reinforced the authority the crowd had already recognised in Jesus as he taught; that was further confirmed by the cure of the centurion's servant which immediately followed it.

These would be important points for the first Christians. But there is a further point about this and other 'cleansings'. The cure brought an excluded person back into the community. Judaism excluded as 'unclean' anyone who was not a Jew. The first Christians rejected such distinctions. In Paul's words, 'Here there cannot be Greek and Jew, circumcised and uncircumcised, barbarian, Scythian, slave, free man, but Christ is all, and in all' (Col 3:11).

Jesus himself was rendered outcast and utterly unclean under Hebrew law when he was condemned to death and crucified. His resurrection was the declaration that no form of uncleanness or exclusion is beyond the power of God's redemptive love. Such a miracle of cleansing as this one is an early pointer to what God was really doing through Jesus.

The woman with an issue of blood (Mt 9:20-33;
Mk 5:25-34; Lk 8:43-48)

The miraculous cure of the woman who had been haemorrhaging for twelve years is recorded in the first three gospels, and occurred when Jesus was under urgent pressure to go to a dying child.

Jesus and the disciples had landed near Capernaum again after a brief stay across the Sea of Galilee when Jesus had exorcised a demoniac. As soon as they reached shore a crowd surrounded them. In the crowd was Jairus, a leading Jew from Capernaum, who pleaded with Jesus to come to the house where his daughter lay dying.

As he hurried after Jairus, surrounded by his disciples and the crowd, Jesus realised 'that power had gone forth from him' (Mk 6:30). He stopped, looked about and asked who had touched him. The disciples pointed out to him that he was being jostled by the crowd, so how could he ask who had touched him? A woman came forward, knelt at Jesus' feet and told him that it was she who had touched Jesus' garments in the hope of being healed.

For twelve years she had suffered from bleeding, and had spent all she possessed seeking a cure. Not only was this physically distressing for her, it also rendered her ritually unclean under Hebrew religious law. The Book of Leviticus, part of the law which Jews believed God had revealed to Moses, ruled that if a woman had a discharge of blood which continued for any lengthy time she was to be considered ritually unclean. Her clothing, bedding and anywhere she sat was also ritually unclean and contaminated anyone who touched any of it. The discharge must stop for seven clear days before she could be considered ritually clean again and have normal social contact with others (Lev 15:25-28).

Jesus said to the woman, 'Daughter, your faith has made you well; go in peace, and be healed of your disease' (Mk 6:34). The word translated 'healed' also means 'saved', and for the first Christians this miracle was a symbol of the salvation they could enjoy through faith in Jesus, as well as the physical healing.

It was also one of the miracles which symbolised that Jesus could overcome conditions which made people outcast or inferior, excluded from membership of privileged groups. This was of vital importance to the first Christians in the rigid social stratifications of their times. The Christian communities of New Testament times included people such as slaves who had little or no prestige or legal rights. Like the 'untouchables' of a rigid caste system, some of them were social outcasts. The saving love of the risen Jesus created a society in which there were no such exclusions.

After healing the woman, Jesus went on to Jairus' house, where he raised his daughter from death (see Chapter 4: 'Resurrection Miracles').

The son of an official at Capernaum (Jn 4:46-54)

The second miracle recorded in John's Gospel is the cure of an official's son at Capernaum in Galilee. Since his first miracle, according to John, when Jesus had turned the water into wine at a wedding feast in Cana, he had been to Jerusalem for the feast of Passover and Unleavened Bread. On that visit he had been angered by the trading in the temple courtyards, and the incident had alerted him to the suspicion he could arouse in the religious authorities. A leading Jew, Nicodemus, had felt he could only approach Jesus secretly and at night for discussions. Although many in Jerusalem had been impressed by him, John records that Jesus did not trust them, 'for he himself knew what was in man' (Jn 2:25).

On the way back to Galilee Jesus and his disciples had passed through Samaria, whose inhabitants were despised by orthodox Jews as heretical and mixed in race. The people of a Samaritan town had readily acknowledged Jesus as Messiah (Jn 4), in contrast to the temple authorities in Jerusalem.

Now he was back in his home region of Galilee again, and while he was visiting Cana a leading Jew came to him from Capernaum. John's Gospel describes him as a 'royal official', probably an administrator appointed by the puppet Jewish ruler of Galilee and Perea, Herod Antipas. The man begged Jesus to come and heal his son, who was near death.

Perhaps Jesus was suspicious of all Jewish officials after his experience in Jerusalem, or he may have thought that Herod Antipas had sent the man to fetch Jesus so that he could entertain him with miracles. (A few hours before Jesus was crucified, Luke's Gospel records that Herod

Antipas wanted him to perform a miracle to satisfy his curiosity, see Lk 23:6-11).

Whatever the reason, Jesus was cautious with the official, and said to him, 'Unless you see signs and wonders you will not believe.'

'Sir, come down before my child dies', the official urgently replied.

'Go,' said Jesus, 'your son will live.'

The man believed what Jesus said, and left (Jn 5:48-50).

On his way home the man was met by servants from his house who told him that his son had recovered. He asked them when it had happened. When they told him, he realised that it was at the time when Jesus had said to him that his son would live.

There are some similarities between this miracle and the cure of the centurion's paralysed servant at Capernaum, but there are also significant differences both in the people involved and in the language. There are also similarities with the resurrection of Jairus' daughter, but again there are marked differences. There is no conclusive reason for thinking that John's Gospel is here recording a version of either of these other miracles.

As the second of the seven 'signs' in John's Gospel before the crucifixion and resurrection of Jesus, the cure of the official's son contributes to the Christian understanding of who Jesus really is. His power is such that he can heal someone at the point of death without being present and merely by command.

But God requires the response of faith from those who need his help, and this response must be given in open trust before a person has experienced any convincing sign of God's power. The official made it clear that he did have the necessary faith. Such faith is trust in God's love made available in Jesus, and is also the response to it. This conviction was central to what the first Christians' were taught to believe about their share in God's love through the risen Jesus, and this miracle would be an important confirmation of their beliefs.

A dropsical man (Lk 14:1-6)

While Jesus was on his way from Galilee to Jerusalem for the last time, Luke's Gospel reports that Jesus had been invited to eat, along with other guests at the house of a Pharisee. His host held an official position and was a man of some importance. Also present – but from what Jesus later said, it was not as a guest – was a man with dropsy, the blood-circulation disorder which causes swollen limbs.

It was a sabbath, and Jesus asked the lawyers and Pharisees present if it was lawful or not to heal on the sabbath. They made no reply. Jesus took the dropsical man, healed him and told him to go. Then he pointedly asked the disapproving religious leaders if they would leave their domestic animals in a well if they fell into one on the sabbath. Again, they made no reply.

Jesus then gave them all some advice about important meals, such as marriage feasts. Guests should take inferior seats rather than vie for the important places, 'For every one who exalts himself will be humbled, and he who humbles himself will be exalted' (Lk 14:11). And he pointedly told the host that he should invite the poor, maimed, lame and blind, who could not repay, rather than his relatives and rich neighbours. He would be repaid at the resurrection of the just, Jesus added.

One of the guests said piously, 'Blessed is he who shall eat bread in the kingdom of God!' (Lk 14:15). In reply Jesus challenged the man with a parable about a marriage feast where all the people invited refused to go because they had more important things to do. So the host sent out for the poor, maimed, blind and lame of the city, the same unfortunates Jesus had just listed to his own host, and then for the destitute. 'For I tell you,' Jesus ended, 'none of those men who were invited shall taste my banquet' (Lk 14:24).

Luke's Gospel emphasises God's special concern for the helpless and disadvantaged. The healing of the dropsical man, followed by Jesus' comments about the behaviour of privileged guests and the parable of the messianic banquet, all placed in sequence, underline this fundamental Christian belief. At first glance the point seems to be that meeting human needs is more important than sabbath observance. But the sequence shows that Jesus is pointing to something more fundamental still, of prime importance for the non-Jewish Christians for which Luke's Gospel was written. Jews treated them as outcasts and excluded them from the synagogues, but God brings them into the messianic community of the new covenant.

Ten lepers (Lk 17:11-19)

At first reading, the account in Luke's Gospel of Jesus healing ten lepers might seem a simple record of a miracle rewarding faith and gratitude. But it is told in a way which emphasises how mistaken the Jews were if they thought that they alone were the real chosen people of God, and that all other peoples, such as the Samaritans, were their inferiors.

As Jesus and his disciples made their last journey to Jerusalem, they entered a village somewhere on the borders of Galilee and Samaria. There Jesus was met by ten lepers, who kept at a distance as the law required, but called out for him to help them. Jesus told them to go and show themselves to the priests, who were responsible in Hebrew law for identifying people with any of the symptoms of leprosy, and for ascertaining that people who lost the symptoms really had been cured.

The ten left Jesus, thus showing that they believed that he had done something for them, and as they went they discovered that their leprosy had gone. Only one of them, when he saw that he was healed, seems to have realised the full extent of what Jesus had done, for he alone returned to Jesus before seeking out the priest. He prostrated himself at the feet of Jesus and thanked him.

The man who returned was a Samaritan, and Jesus asked whether he was the only one to be cured: 'Were not ten cleansed? Where are the nine? Was no one found to return and give praise to God except this foreigner?' (Lk 17:17-18). Then he told the man to get up and go on his way, and that his faith had made him well. There is no mention of what actually happened to the other nine; the account of the miracle concentrates on the gratitude to Jesus expressed by the one who returned, and the assurances Jesus gave him.

Written after the first Christian Churches had expanded far beyond Palestine and drawn many non-Jews into their membership, Luke's Gospel emphasises the saving role of Jesus for all, but particularly for people treated by others as inferior.

The high priest's slave (Lk 22:50-51)

It is ironic that the miracle Jesus performed in the very last moments of his freedom, as he was being arrested, should be for one of the officials sent by the high priest to arrest him.

As the Jewish officials and soldiers sent by the high priest arrived in the Garden of Gethsemane to arrest Jesus late on the Thursday night, confusion broke out. They needed to be sure which one was Jesus, so Judas stepped forward to greet him with a kiss, the sign of identification which Judas had agreed with the authorities. When they saw what was happening, Jesus' disciples began to fight the men sent to arrest him.

Peter drew a sword, slashed at one of the officials and cut off his right ear. Ordering his disciples to stop fighting, Jesus touched the wounded man and healed him. Then he asked the men in charge of the arrest why they had waited until now, and come so heavily armed, when they could have taken him any time they wanted while he was teaching in the temple courtyards. They made no reply, but just took Jesus away to the high priest's house for questioning.

There are no more miracles before the death of Jesus, despite everyone's expectations that he would show his powers to save himself and convince his accusers that he really was the Messiah. Within eighteen hours of healing one of his enemies, Jesus was being crucified. He accepted that appalling outcome, and died.

The significance of these miracles

These miracles, scattered throughout his ministry from its earliest days to its very end at the moment of his arrest, show how wide a range of people Jesus helped. They include lepers, who could be of any social class but were outcast by reason of their disease, a sick and deprived man watching the wealthy and influencial guests at a formal meal, a royal official and an official of the high priest's household.

This range of people helped by Jesus would be particularly significant for the first Christians, for their communities were composed of people of all classes who were united only by their faith in the power of the risen Jesus.

Most significant of all would be the healing miracles in which Jesus overcame a disability – leprosy or an issue of blood – which rendered the sufferer unclean under Hebrew religious law and excluded them from normal society. Nor were the Jews unusual in this respect; most societies then, as now, were composed of groups which considered others to be their inferiors and socially unacceptable.

Early in the history of the apostolic missions, according to the Acts of the Apostles, Peter was criticised by some of the Christians of Jerusalem who were still keeping the exclusive Hebrew ritual laws in which they had been nurtured. They disapproved of Peter staying with non-Jews in the course of his missionary work.

Peter was able to counter their criticisms by telling them about a vision he had received. He had seen a great sheet being lowered by its corners from heaven, containing the 'unclean' animals which Hebrew law forbade as food. A voice told Peter to kill and eat, and when he objected to doing this the voice said, 'What God has cleansed you must not call common' (Acts 11:9). In this sense the Greek word translated 'common' also means 'inferior', just as 'common' does in English.

But just as with 'common', the Greek word is also the root of the words for 'community' and 'communion'. Then as now, the Christian community was composed of many whom the rest of the world considered inferior and unfit for their society, but in God's eyes they were members of his kingdom and his sons and daughters. Indeed, the poorer and more despised they were by earthly standards, the more privileged they were in God's eyes.

8

Exorcisms of demons

Miracle	Matthew	Mark	Luke	John
Demonic possession				
The man in a synagogue in Capernaum		1:23-28	4:33-37	
The man or men of Gerasa	8:28-34	5:1-20	8:26-39	
The Canaanite woman's daughter	15:21-28	7:24-30		
The epileptic boy	17:14-17	9:14-21	9:37-43	
A dumb man	9:32-33		11:14	
A blind and dumb man	12:22			
The woman bent double in a synagogue			13:10-17	
(Mary Magdalene		16:9	8:2)	

The gospels give detailed accounts of seven miracles performed by Jesus in which he expels 'demons' or 'devils' from people possessed by them. Two of the gospels also mention that he had cast out seven demons from Mary Magdalene but they do not give any details nor say when it happened.

The gospel accounts of the miracles distinguish between healings in which there is no mention of demonic possession and healings which result from exorcism. It can be misleading to make too much of this distinction, but it is clear that the people of the gospels, including Jesus himself, firmly believed that people could be possessed by personal forces of evil and gravely harmed by them. Some of the official Jewish religious groups accused Jesus himself of being possessed by the highest of diabolical powers, which gave him the power to subdue lesser demons (Mt 12:24; Mk 3:22).

Such beliefs are often dismissed today, and claims of demonic possession are explained as extreme cases of compulsive psychological conditions where the victims have little or no control over their actions. Some theories combine both kinds of explanation, by holding that demons are more easily able to take possession of people with impaired personalities, and exacerbate their symptoms.

The power of imagination plays an important part in accepting or dismissing belief in demons and demonic powers. Conventional images of small red imps with leathery skins, forked tails and pitchforks, or of dark, majestically winged figures with flashing eyes, only make it more difficult to think clearly about the problem of personal evil. But whatever the underlying beliefs may be, the range of exorcisms described in the gospels make it clear that no evil is so powerful, or personality disorder so deep, that it can resist Jesus' power to overcome it.

The man in the synagogue in Capernaum (Mk 1:23-28; Lk 4:33-37)

The first miracle of Jesus' ministry reported by Mark and Luke occurred on a sabbath in the synagogue at Capernaum, where Jesus went to live at the beginning of his public ministry. Situated at the northern end of the Sea of Galilee just west of where the River Jordan enters it, Capernaum was quite an important small town on the main route from Mesopotamia to Palestine. The surrounding countryside was fertile, there was a customs post and a Roman garrison, and it was the base for boats fishing the Sea of Galilee. The first four disciples, Simon (Peter), Andrew, James and John lived in Capernaum. Jesus made it his home base for most of his ministry until he set out on his final journey to Jerusalem.

Jesus was not an official teacher, but any Jewish man could speak in a synagogue by arrangement with the president, and Mark gives the impression that this exorcism occurred on the first occasion that Jesus taught there. He made a deep impression on the people present, and Mark says that they drew an unfavourable comparison between Jesus and the official religious teachers: 'They were astonished at his teaching, for he taught them as one who had authority, and not as the scribes' (Mk 1:22).

Suddenly, a man in the congregation began to shout at Jesus that 'they' wanted nothing to do with him and asking if he had come to destroy them. Mark explains that the man was under the control of an 'unclean spirit', Luke says an 'unclean devil', which then told Jesus that it knew who he was, 'the Holy One of God' (Mk 1:24).

Jesus rebuked the spirit, told it to be silent and ordered it to come out. The spirit then left the man, injuring him as it did so and crying out. The people present were amazed by the event and treated it as a new dimension to the authority of Jesus. Not only did he teach with greater authority than others but even the unclean spirits obeyed him. His reputation spread throughout the region.

As the first miracle reported by Mark and Luke, placed so soon after the account of the temptations, it is vivid evidence that Jesus could defeat the power of Satan as well as resist it. Moreover, Mark says that Jesus opened his public ministry with the claim, 'The time is fulfilled, and the kingdom of God is at hand' (Mk 1:15), while Luke reports that Jesus performed this exorcism in Capernaum immediately after being rejected in his home-town of Nazareth. There, Jesus had quoted one of the prophecies of Isaiah foretelling the age of the Messiah, and had applied it to himself, but they could not believe that their local 'Joseph's son' could possibly be the Messiah.

The Capernaum expulsion of an evil spirit which had identified Jesus as 'the Holy One of God' confirmed his claims at the beginning of his ministry. Like so many of his miracles, Jesus had suddenly been confronted with a situation demanding action, and he had shown that he could instantly call on his messianic power. The kingdom of God had come.

The man or men of Gerasa (The Gerasene swine)
(Mt 8:28-34; Mk 5:1-20; Lk 8:26-39)

The next exorcism of which the first three gospels give a detailed description was even more dramatic. Mark's Gospel sets the incident on the day following the exorcism at Capernaum. The previous evening Jesus had healed and exorcised the throngs of sick and possessed people brought to him, and then he and his disciples had taken to boats to cross the Sea of Galilee and escape from the crowds. During the voyage they had been overtaken by a storm, but Jesus had quelled it and they had landed safely on the furthest shores at the southern end.

They had come to the northern border of a large region called the Decapolis, the 'Ten Towns', most of which lay east of the River Jordan between the Sea of Galilee and the Dead Sea. The region was a result of the cosmopolitan history of Palestine. Old towns had been annexed by Alexander the Great and settled by Greek veterans; the Jews took them over when they threw off Greek rule; then the Romans freed them from the Jews and gave the towns self-government within the Roman province of Syria. The inhabitants of the ten towns had formed a league for trade and defence, and the herd of pigs shows how free they were from Jewish law.

When Jesus and the disciples landed they were confronted by a maniac, naked and trailing the broken fetters by which his fellow townsmen had tried to restrain him. Crying out, and scarred by self-inflicted wounds, he found what shelter he could away from the towns amongst the tombs of a graveyard.

As soon as he saw Jesus he ran to him and threw himself

at his feet. Jesus ordered the unclean spirit to come out of the man, but it replied in words similar to those of the demoniac in the synagogue at Capernaum: 'What have you to do with me, Jesus, Son of the Most High God? I adjure you, by God, do not torment me' (Mk 5:7). Jesus asked it its name, the traditional way of showing authority over someone. It replied that its name was 'Legion', perhaps indicating that it was a colony of spirits as numerous as a Roman legion, and asked to go into a nearby herd of pigs rather than be sent far away.

Jesus consented. The evil spirits entered the pigs and the whole herd rushed to its death down a steep slope into the nearby Sea of Galilee. The herdsmen fled to tell everyone what had happened. A crowd gathered and saw the possessed man sitting calmly, clothed and sane. The herdsmen repeated what they had seen and the people begged Jesus to go away from their neighbourhood.

As Jesus and the disciples began to get back into their boats the exorcised man asked if he could go with them, but Jesus told him to go home to his friends and tell them what had been done for him. The miracle had been done outside Jewish territory, so there was little danger that the publicity would harm Jesus' mission.

The incident points to the belief that evil spirits could not survive on their own but had to inhabit some living thing, and there may also be overtones of the Jewish prohibition of pork as an 'unclean' food. But within the gospel account of Jesus, it shows that he has complete power over evil spirits no matter how numerous they may be.

The Canaanite woman's daughter (Mk 7:24-30)

The expulsion of demonic forces near Gerasa, described above, occurred in the Decapolis which Jews claimed was part of the Promised Land which should be under Jewish rule. The exorcism of the Canaanite woman's daughter shows Jesus exercising his power over evil at a distance to reach a girl in Tyre, a territory which had never been Jewish.

Both Matthew's and Mark's Gospels present this exorcism immediately after a fierce controversy between Jesus and a group of Pharisees and scribes from Jerusalem. The Pharisees believed in strict observance of the complex details of the Jewish religious laws, and the scribes were the specialists in recording and interpreting the text of the Jewish religious books, particularly the five books of the law.

Jesus was teaching that the spirit of the law was more important – and more demanding – than the letter of it, and his religious opponents had noted that he and his disciples did not bother with the complex ritual of washing prescribed before eating. Jesus roundly accused them of hypocrisy. They scrupulously observed human traditions, he said, but ignored far more serious obligations, laid down by God, by resorting to spurious legal arguments.

Jesus then withdrew to a house in the north where Galilee bordered on the region of Tyre and Sidon, to escape from the growing hostility of the Jewish religious officials.

There a Greek woman from the Tyre region found him, fell at his feet and asked him to expel a devil possessing her daughter.

Jesus replied that his mission was to his fellow Jews, not to Gentiles, and told her that the children must be fed first. Until that had been done, he said, it was not right to give the children's food to the puppies. There is no point in trying to tone down Jesus' answer. It was clear to him from the opposition he was arousing that he could not afford to expand his mission outside his own people. Jews must receive him as Messiah before he could turn to the Gentiles, because God had chosen the Hebrews to be the bridgehead for his messianic mission to the world.

But the woman would not be dismissed. She accepted his point, but riposted, 'Yes, Lord; yet even the puppies eat the crumbs that fall from their master's table' (Mt 15:27). Jesus commended her great faith, and commanded that what she wanted should be done. When she reached home she found that her child was well again.

The incident shows that Jesus could subdue evil even

when he was not physically present. It also shows that whatever the tactics of his mission might have to be, his messianic power to save was not confined to the Jews. Both of these points would be vitally important to the first Christians as the early Church expanded beyond its Jewish and Palestinian base into the other Mediterranean countries, where its members were predominantly Gentile. The Messiah's mission of healing and salvation, and his divine authority, extend into all the world.

Paul's missions almost invariably began in the Jewish synagogues of the Greek towns he visited, but he then reached out to the non-Jewish citizens to found the local Churches. This story of the exorcism of a Gentile girl outside the Jewish homeland would be immensely important to such Gentile congregations. The Hebrew bridgehead had served its purpose with the death and resurrection of Jesus; the new order of messianic salvation was already spreading far beyond its Hebrew origins.

The epileptic boy (Mt 17:14-17; Mk 9:10-21; Lk 9:37-43)

One of the great turning points in the gospel story is the transfiguration, when Jesus took Peter, James and John to a hilltop and they saw him clothed in dazzling garments talking to Moses and Elijah.

The four descended from that moment of glory to a scene of chaos. They found the remaining disciples in the centre of a large crowd arguing with scribes. As soon as the crowd saw Jesus they ran to him and he asked them what the argument was about. One of the crowd told him that he had brought his son to the disciples to be healed but they had been unable to do anything for him.

The symptoms the man described match those of epilepsy.

When the fits were upon him the boy fell to the ground, foamed at the mouth, ground his teeth and became rigid. The man attributed it to possession of the boy by a 'dumb spirit' (Mk 9:17).

Jesus' first reaction was one of weary sadness that no one seemed to have learned anything about the nature of faith from his teaching; his criticism included everyone present, his disciples, the scribes and the crowd. He asked them how long they expected him to be with them and bear with them, and told them to bring the boy to him.

As soon as he arrived the boy had another fit: 'When the spirit saw him, immediately it convulsed the boy, and he fell on the ground and rolled about, foaming at the mouth.' The boy's father said that this had been happening since his son was an infant and he had often fallen into the fire or into water to the danger of his life. 'If you can do anything,' he concluded, 'have pity on us and help us' (Mk 9:20-22).

Jesus echoed the man's words, 'If you can!' and added, 'All things are possible to him who believes.' The father immediately replied that he did believe, but asked Jesus to help his 'unbelief' (Mk 9:23-24). Although he does believe that Jesus can help, he is afraid that his belief is not strong enough to work the miracle needed.

The boy's father need not have feared. Jesus ordered the spirit to leave the boy and never to return. The boy was thrown into an even worse fit and lay as if dead, but Jesus took his hand, lifted him to his feet and showed that the boy was healed.

When his disciples later asked Jesus why they had been unable to do anything for the boy, he told them that this kind of evil could only be defeated by prayer, and some of the ancient gospel manuscripts add fasting as well, implying that the disciples still had far to go in their understanding of prayer and their practice of it.

The incident is also important for the light it throws on faith. If faith is trust in Jesus, it can still be an effective response to the love and power of God, even though the 'faithful' are conscious of how inadequate their faith really is. On the evidence of Paul's letter to the Romans, the first Christians understood that the Holy Spirit amplified their response of faith, so that it could be a truly adequate response to the love of God. They believed that they were children of

God in the fullest sense, through their share in the Holy
Spirit and of the sonship of Christ (e.g. Rom 5:1-5; 8:15-17),
so they could relate to the Father as fully as the Holy Spirit
and Jesus Christ himself.

A dumb man; and a blind and dumb man
(Mt 9:32-33; Lk 11:14; and Mt 12:22)

Two exorcisms, the first of a dumb man recorded by in
Matthew's and Luke's Gospels, and the second of a blind
and dumb man recorded only by Matthew, are remarkable
for the damning explanation the religious authorities gave to
explain Jesus powers over evil.

By the time these incidents occurred, Jesus' reputation as
a teacher, exorcist and healer had spread throughout Galilee.
Jesus tried to make people keep silent about his miracles
within Jewish territory because of extremist and nationalist
beliefs about the Messiah. He must educate people,
particularly his twelve disciples, to understand his
messiahship in his way, not the popular way.

Under Luke's arrangement of the gospel material, Jesus
had already left Galilee and begun his last journey to
Jerusalem to proclaim his messianic claims openly and
compel the religious leaders to decide one way or the other.
This is significant for what happened at these two exorcisms
on the way.

Both of them are straightforward incidents. In the first a
dumb man was brought to him 'possessed with a devil'.
Jesus cast the evil spirit out, the dumb man spoke and the
crowd marvelled. In the second incident the possessed man
was blind as well as dumb. Jesus healed him, the man spoke
and saw, and the crowds acclaimed Jesus with the messianic
title 'Son of David'.

But on both occasions there were Pharisees present,
members of the powerful religious party which took offence
at Jesus lax attitude towards the details of the law. It was
essential for them to explain Jesus' powers of exorcism to

the crowds, but the explanation must avoid confirming his claims as Messiah.

They decided that Jesus' powers were themselves satanic, and more diabolical than any evil spirit he might encounter. He could therefore force all other evil spirits to obey him as their superior in evil: 'It is only by Beelzebul, the prince of demons, that this man casts out demons' (Mt 12:22). Mark's Gospel records that this explanation was also being circulated by the scribes.

Jesus riposted that Satan's rule must indeed have ended if his kingdom was so divided against itself. But he went on to say that such an accusation was an unforgivable sin, and indeed that it was the only unforgivable sin, because it asserted that the Holy Spirit was evil. If people really believed that, they could interpret every act of God's love as an evil deception, and they would be beyond God's reach. Nothing Jesus did would now convince them, because it could all be dismissed as satanically evil. If they were determined to misinterpret God's love, expressed by Jesus, as the manifestation of supreme evil, they would never be able to respond to it. Such a belief was the antithesis of faith.

The woman bent double in a synagogue (Lk 13:10-17)

A little further on during the journey to Jerusalem in Luke's account, Jesus performed another exorcism which provoked a protest, this time from the president of a synagogue.

Once again, Jesus had been invited to teach at the sabbath day meeting of local Jews. One of the people present was a woman who had been crippled for many years by 'a spirit of infirmity' which bent her double. When Jesus saw her he called her to him from the area of the synagogue reserved for women, told her that she was freed from the infirmity and laid his hands on her. She was immediately able to stand straight and she praised God for what had been done for her.

The president of the synagogue decided that the exorcism broke the sabbath legislation. He angrily told those present, 'There are six days on which work ought to be done; come on those days and be healed, and not on the sabbath day' (Lk 13:14). The legislation protecting the sabbath, the seventh day of the week, is enacted in the most sacred part of Hebrew law as one of the Ten Commandments (Ex 20:1-17; Deut 5:7-21), and forbids any work being done.

Jesus silenced his critics just as firmly with an accusation of hypocrisy. They all loosed their animals from their stalls to get water whether it was the sabbath or not, he said. This woman, he continued, this daughter of Abraham, had been bound by Satan for eighteen years; should she not be loosed from her restriction on the sabbath?

The sabbath legislation gives two reasons for the sanctity of the day: it is a celebration of the day when God rested after the six days of creation, the day for contemplating the perfection of God's creative work; and it celebrates the exodus from Egypt when God overcame the Egyptians and released the Hebrew people from their slavery. Both of these motives for celebration are implicit in this exorcism. Jesus released the woman from the evil which held her, and restored her to the health God intended for all his creation. The sabbath was an appropriate day on which to do it.

Mary Magdalene (Mk 16:9; Lk 8:2)

Two of the gospels, Mark's and Luke's, mention that Mary Magdalene had been exorcised by Jesus of seven demons, but neither of them gives any details of where it happened, nor at what point in his ministry Jesus did the miracle. The reference in Mark occurs in that gospel's last block of material, 16:9-20, which there are good reasons for thinking was added to this gospel by a later hand.

Luke's Gospel, on the other hand, mentions it during a summary about Jesus Galilean ministry, when Mary Magdalene and two other women are listed as accompanying

Jesus and the twelve disciples as he travelled through the cities and villages of Galilee 'preaching and bringing the good news of the kingdom of God' (Lk 8:1).

The gospels record that Mary Magdalene was present on three more occasions. She was one of the women who stood by the cross of Jesus during his crucifixion; she saw Jesus being buried and stayed to keep watch for a while over the sealed tomb; and she was one of the three women who went to the tomb early on the third day (a sabbath had intervened) to anoint the body of Jesus. They found the tomb empty, and subsequently Mary Magdalene was the first person to see the risen Jesus and speak with him (Jn 20:14-17).

Although Mary Magdalene has been traditionally identified with the woman whose sins Jesus forgave in the house of Simon the Pharisee (Lk 7:36-50), there is no evidence for thinking that this woman was in fact Mary Magdalene. If she were, it is surprising that Luke's Gospel does not make the connection when she is listed so soon afterwards (8:1).

The significance of the exorcisms

The public work of Jesus began with his baptism, in which the voice from heaven proclaimed him God's beloved Son, and his temptations, when he successfully withstood the power of evil, referred to in the gospel accounts as Satan or the devil. At the end of his ministry, immediately before his arrest in the Garden of Gethsemane, Jesus said to the chief priests, the captains of the temple and the elders who had all come to take him, 'this is your hour and the power of darkness' (Lk 22:53). The first Christians believed that the sufferings and crucifixion of Jesus were a further confrontation between God and the spiritual powers of supreme evil. The resurrection of Jesus was therefore the visible evidence that God's love is more powerful than all evil, and that this power is available to all who believe in the risen and ascended Christ.

106

The selection of exorcism miracles in the gospels is designed to explain what this means in practice for Christians who trust in God's love and share its power through their union with Christ and the Holy Spirit. The incidents show him overcoming evil in personal form which acknowledges who he is, and multiple evil present in strength. He overcomes evil amongst Gentiles and Jews alike, both near and at a distance. He overcomes evil which has defeated all other efforts to dislodge it, even the efforts of his own disciples. His power over evil stems from God, not from a more evil power than the evil he encounters, and Jesus is not subject to the restrictions of human religious traditions, even of the highest authority, in his exercise of his powers.

The gospel records of these miracles gave great comfort to people who felt that they lived in a world dominated by manifold forms of personal evil. Their God, become incarnate in Jesus, was the one supreme God, who must be obeyed by every other power, visible or invisible, good or evil, spiritual or earthly. It meant that their redemption gave them practical protection from anything they might fear, even while they were sharing in the sufferings of Christ so as to share his glory.

9

The four gospels and their miracles

It is fascinating to compare the four gospels with each other to see what each of them includes or leaves out, and to find how each of them arranges its material. Such a study suggests that the four gospels were originally compiled for four different groups, each with different backgrounds and needs: Matthew's Gospel for Jewish Christians in Palestine; Mark's Gospel for Christians in Rome; Luke's Gospel for non-Jewish Greek-speaking Christians in the eastern Mediterranean, where Paul had travelled; and John's Gospel for Jewish Christians outside Palestine who needed to defend their beliefs about Jesus against other religions popular in their region.

No one would claim to know exactly when each gospel was written, so giving them dates only conveys an idea of their probable sequence and of roughly how much time had elapsed since the death of Jesus. Moreover, 'written' only refers to the final stage in their formation, when they were edited into the form that we now have. There would be a number of collections of material about Jesus circulating among the early Christians before the information was finalised as the four gospels, and some of these collections may even have been in written form. But we cannot know for sure, because only the final editions of the four gospels have survived.

Three of them, Matthew, Mark and Luke, seem to use a lot of the same information about Jesus and to present it in much the same language. A closer examination of them shows that Matthew and Luke contain most of the information that is in Mark. Matthew and Luke also contain information which is in both of them but not in Mark. Finally, Matthew contains information which does not appear in any other gospel, and so too does Luke.

The most widely accepted explanation for all this is that Mark's Gospel was the first to be written down, about thirty-five years after the crucifixion. Matthew and Luke used Mark's Gospel – or the same information that Mark had used – but they added to it in two ways. First they both added more information from a source that Mark had not used. Then they each of them added material which no other gospel used. This can be seen most clearly in the stories about the birth and childhood of Jesus. Matthew provides information which is not found anywhere else, and so does Luke; the contents of the two gospels are quite different in those early chapters, and Mark does not record anything at all about the birth and childhood of Jesus.

We are familiar with the sequence of gospels as they appear in the New Testament: Matthew, Mark, Luke and John. Bearing in mind what material they actually contain, it is more likely that Mark came first, then Matthew and Luke about ten years later. Finally, John's Gospel was written later still, and presents a very developed view of who Jesus was, perhaps based on many years of spiritual reflection on what he did and said.

THE MIRACLES IN MATTHEW'S GOSPEL

The author of Matthew thinks like a Jewish rabbi, and emphasises the aspects of Jesus which would appeal most to Christians with a strongly Jewish background. Jesus is shown as the new Moses, who reveals a deeper attitude towards the divine law (see Mt 5:20-48). He is the Messiah who fulfils all the promises of the Old Testament (see the list of his ancestry in Mt 1:1-17, and compare it with Lk 3:23-38!). He is the king of the new kingdom of God, the new King David (the first effective Hebrew king), but Jesus' kingdom is not a political kingdom and it does not have territorial limits.

Much of this may be summed up in a passage (most of which is unique to Matthew) from the Sermon on the Mount:

> Do not think that I have come to abolish the law and the prophets. I have come not to abolish them but to fulfil them. For truly, I say to you, till heaven and earth pass away, not an iota, not a dot, will pass from the law until all is accomplished' (Mt 5:17-18).

As we have seen, Matthew's Gospel is best understood as a work composed of material from Mark's Gospel, to which is added extra material also used by Luke, as well as material which only appears in Matthew. All this information about Jesus was then reshaped by the editor for Christians who had been brought up as strict Jews. Like the rest of the New Testament, Matthew was written in Greek, but there may have been an earlier edition in Hebrew or Aramaic; if there was, it has not survived and we do not know just what it contained.

A conspicuous feature of this gospel consists of five different collections of material from the teaching of Jesus, arranged as discourses or sermons. Each of these discourses contains sayings and parables of Jesus dealing with a different topic, and they may well have been collections of material which circulated among the early Christian Churches before the four gospels were written.

The first of these discourses, the Sermon on the Mount, contains the kind of teaching Jesus gave to show what really makes people important in the eyes of God, and to teach his followers about the new attitudes they should have about the Hebrew law and their relations with other people. The second is a collection of parables; the third discourse is a collection of instructions by Jesus to disciples; the fourth collects together some of Jesus' teaching about the way to govern a Christian community. Finally there is a collection of Jesus' teaching about the end of the world and the judgement.

Structure   (The five discourses of Jesus are underlined)

1:1 - 2:23   THE BIRTH AND INFANCY OF JESUS

3:1 - 7:29   JESUS BEGINS HIS MINISTRY
                   A: Narrative Section (3:1 - 4:25)
                      The baptism and temptations of Jesus
                   B: The Sermon on the Mount (5:1 - 7:29)

8:1 - 10:42   THE APOSTLES ARE COMMISSIONED
                   A: Narrative Section: (8:1 - 9:37)
                      Ten Miracles
                   B: Instructions for apostles (10:1-42)

11:1 -13:52   ASPECTS OF THE KINGDOM OF HEAVEN
                   A: Narrative Section (11:1 - 12:50)
                      Various miracles and incidents
                   B: Discourse of parables (13:1-52)

13:53 - 18:35   THE CHURCH
                   A: Narrative Section (13:53 - 17:27)
                      Miracles and conflicts
                      Peter's recognition of Jesus as Messiah
                      The transfiguration
                   B: The discourse on the Church (18:1-35)

19:1 - 25:46   APPROACHING SUFFERINGS AND TRIALS
                   A: Narrative Section (19:1 - 23:39)
                      Conflicts, prophecies and a miracle
                      The triumphal entry into Jerusalem
                      Controversies in the temple
                   B: The end and second coming (24:1 - 25:46)

26:1 - 28:20   THE PASSION AND RESURRECTION
                   The Passover Meal
                   The Garden of Gethsemane
                   The arrest
                   Jesus' trial before the Sanhedrin
                   Peter's denials
                   Jesus' trial before Pilate

THE CRUCIFIXION AND DEATH OF JESUS
The burial
THE EMPTY TOMB
Jesus appears to the women
Jesus appears to his disciples in Galilee

How, then, does Matthew's Gospel use the miracles of Jesus in its presentation of the life and teaching of Jesus? Like the other three gospels, the author of Matthew selects only some of the miracles he knew Jesus had performed, and then he arranges them to serve his general purpose and his readers' interests. But first, a reminder of which miracles are recorded in Matthew's Gospel, and the order in which they appear. The following list also gives the references to the parallel passages in the other three gospels.

The miracles in Matthew's Gospel

Title	Type	Matthew	Mark	Luke	John
A leper	H&P	8:1-4	1:40-45	5:12-16	
The centurion's servant	H	8:5-13	7:1-10		
Peter's mother-in-law	H	8:14-15	1:29-31	4:38-39	
The storm stilled	N	8:23-27	4:35-41	8:22-25	
The men of Gerasa	E	8:28-34	5:1-20	8:26-39	
A paralysed man in Capernaum	H	9:1-8	2:1-12	5:17-26	
Jairus' daughter	R	9:18-26	5:21-43	8:40-56	
The woman with an issue of blood	H&P	9:20-22	5:23-34	8:43-48	
Two blind men	H	9:27-31			
A dumb man	E	9:32-33		11:14	
A man with a withered hand	H	12:9-14	3:1-6	6:6-11	
A blind and dumb man	E	12:22			
Feeding the 5000	N	14:13-21	6:30-44	9:10-17	6:1-14
Walking on water	N	14:22-33	6:45-52		6:16-21
The Canaanite woman's daughter	E	15:21-28	7:24-30		

Title	Type	Matthew	Mark	Luke	John
Feeding the 4000	N	15:32-39	8:1-10		
The epileptic boy	E	17:14-17	9:14-21	9:37-43	
The coin in a fish's mouth	N	17:24-27			
Blind Bartimaeus	H	20:29-34	10:46-52	18:35-43	
A fig tree cursed	N	21:18-22	11:12-14, 20-24		

Key: E: Exorcism; H: Healing; N: Nature; P: Purification; R: Resurrection.

The most conspicuous example of the way Matthew's Gospel uses the selected miracles comes immediately after the Sermon on the Mount, when this gospel immediately presents the reader with a series of ten miracles. That discourse shows Jesus setting out the uncompromising ideals by which his followers must live. The people of the new covenant must go far beyond the letter of the old Hebrew law; they must keep its spirit and fulfil the ideals it was meant to express and guard. They must be as perfect as their Father in heaven, said Jesus. When the sermon ended, the people exclaimed that Jesus spoke with unique authority, unlike the Jewish religious leaders.

Christians with a Jewish background who read or heard that passage would recognise it immediately as the fulfilment of their old Hebrew religion. But are such ideals practicable? The ten miracles which immediately follow demonstrate that Jesus has the power to calm storms, to cure people, to heal impaired human faculties, to exorcise evil, to cleanse the unclean and restore them to their communities, and even to raise the dead to life again. That is Matthew's proof that Jesus can overcome anything which hinders the realisation of the ideals he taught.

The Old Testament prophets had promised that God would bring in a new covenant, when the law would be inscribed on his people's hearts so that they really could respond to him and fulfil his ideals. The Sermon on the Mount sets out the law of that new covenant. The first Christians believed that the risen Jesus shared his powers with them, and the miracles show what that power can do for them. The miracles also show the need to respond with faith to God's demonstration of love, but they now have the evidence that such a response is practicable; the full life of God's love is within their reach.

The next two miracles, the healing of the man with the withered hand and of the blind and dumb man, both concentrate not on the healings themselves but on the criticism of Jesus by Pharisees for healing people on a sabbath. They are set in the midst of a number of rejection incidents, when the Pharisees, rigid guardians of the letter of the old Hebrew law, criticise Jesus for technical breaches of the sabbath law. Jesus told them plainly that the messianic Son of man was Lord of the sabbath.

The next group of miracles consists of six set in the narrative section which builds up to the discourse on the Church. This is the collection of Jesus' teachings about the way members of the new covenant community should treat each other.

The two feedings, of crowds of 5000 and of 4000, with their eucharistic pattern of Jesus taking, blessing, breaking and distributing the food, have symbolism which relates the first of them to Jews and the second of them to Gentiles. The new community transcends the old Hebrew beliefs that the covenant people of God are separate from Gentiles. At the death of Jesus Matthew's Gospel reports that the veil of the Hebrew temple, symbol of exclusion, split from top to bottom.

The power at work in such feedings is demonstrated by Jesus walking on water, with its echo of the mysterious power operating at the creation of the world and at the escape of the Hebrews from Egypt. Jesus' exorcism of the Canaanite woman's daughter shows that his mission is also to foreigners if they have faith in Jesus and recognise that it is he who provides the 'children's bread'. The creative power of God which the rigidly conservative Jews thought was their exclusive privilege is now universally available.

Finally in this group, comes first the exorcism and cure of the epileptic boy by Jesus after his disciples had failed. Jesus told them that they had failed because they lacked faith. The miracles emphasise that Jesus alone has the faith and power to defeat evil and to give salvation. The Church will fail unless it depends solely on the principles and power of Jesus. Then the miracle of the coin in the fish's mouth, which Jesus used to pay tax, demonstrates that Jesus recognises the place of the secular authorities; so too must the Church.

Finally, there are two miracles set either side of Jesus' final entry into Jerusalem as the Messiah and his expulsion of the traders from the temple. These are the healing of two blind men and the withering of the fig tree.

The blind men address Jesus as ' Lord', the Old Testament title for God, and as 'Son of David', the messianic title. Jesus healed them and they followed him. The crowds who welcomed Jesus into Jerusalem also addressed him as Son of David. But only Matthew reports that the crowds in the temple also shouted that Jesus was Son of David as he drove the traders out.

Against this background, the fig tree which failed to provide fruit when Jesus looked for it is a clear symbol of the failure of the Hebrew religion to fulfil its covenant responsibilities, and particularly the failure of the religious authorities to recognise Jesus as Messiah.

In its early years the infant Christian Church had to make the momentous decision of whether it should break with Judaism. It did so, but throughout the New Testament period there were groups of Christians who argued that all Christians – even Gentile Christians – must keep the full Hebrew religious law. For Christians who had been faithful Jews, Matthew's Gospel presented Jesus as the fulfilment of their old faith and also as its replacement. The way this gospel presents the miracles of Jesus reinforces this Christian belief. It may also have helped Christians with Jewish backgrounds in their defence against the Jewish religious authorities when they were expelled from the synagogues or brought before the official religious courts.

THE MIRACLES IN MARK'S GOSPEL

Compared with the other three gospels, Mark's Gospel appears to have a much less complex structure: a series of incidents from the life and teaching of Jesus arranged around a small number of key events. The gospel begins with only the minimum of introduction, amounting to little more than a title, then goes straight to the baptism of Jesus. There is nothing about Jesus' birth, infancy or childhood. At the end of the gospel there is very little information about events following the resurrection of Jesus. This makes for a narrative with a very direct impact, and although it is shorter than the other gospels it usually provides more information about the incidents it does report.

Key events in Mark's Gospel

1:9	The baptism and temptations
8:27	Peter's declaration that Jesus is the Messiah
9:2	The transfiguration
11:1	The triumphal entry into Jerusalem
11:15	Jesus goes to the temple
14:22	The Lord's Supper
14:32	Jesus prays in Gethsemane
14:44	The arrest
14:53	Jesus before the Jewish Great Council at night
15:1	Jesus before the Council again, in the morning
15:2	Jesus before the regional Roman magistrate, Pontius Pilate
15:6	Pilate sentences Jesus to death
15:24	The crucifixion
15:33	The death of Jesus
16:1	The resurrection

The miracles in Mark's Gospel

Title	Type	Matthew	**Mark**	Luke	John
The man in the synagogue in Capernaum	E		**1:23-28**	4:33-37	
Peter's mother-in-law	H	8:14-15	**1:29-31**	4:38-39	
A Leper	H&P	8:1-4	**1:40-45**	5:12-16	
A paralysed man in Capernaum	H	9:1-8	**2:1-12**	5:17-26	
A man with a withered hand	H	12:9-14	**3:1-6**	6:6-11	
The storm stilled	N	8:23-27	**4:35-41**	8:22-25	
A man of Gerasa	E	8:28-34	**5:1-20**	8:26-39	
Jairus' daughter	R	9:18-26	**5:21-43**	8:40-56	
The woman with an issue of blood	H&P	9:20-22	**5:23-34**	8:43-48	
Feeding the 5000	N	14:13-21	**6:30-44**	9:10-17	6:1-14
Walking on water	N	14:22-33	**6:45-52**		6:16-21
The centurion's servant	H	8:5-13	**7:1-10**		
A Canaanite woman's daughter	E	15:21-28	**7:24-30**		
A deaf-mute	H		**7:31-37**		
Feeding the 4000	N	15:32-39	**8:1-10**		
A blind man at Bethsaida	H		**8:22-26**		
The epileptic boy	E	17:14-17	**9:14-21**	9:37-43	
Blind Bartimaeus	H	20:29-34	**10:46-52**	18:35-43	
A fig tree cursed	N	21:18-22	**11:12-14, 20-24**		

Key: E: Exorcism; H: Healing; N: Nature; P: Purification; R: Resurrection.

From these two lists it can be seen that Peter's confession of faith in Jesus and the transfiguration form a decisive turning point in the gospel. By far the greatest proportion of the miracles, seventeen of them, are placed before these two connected events and one follows immediately as comment on them. Only two remain, and these are both of them closely associated with Jesus' triumphal entry into Jerusalem.

As we have seen, Mark's Gospel was probably the first of the four to be edited or written in the form we now have, and it is equally probable that Matthew and Luke drew on Mark's material for their own gospels. It is not possible to tell, therefore, how Mark adapted the sources he used to meet the needs of his particular group of Christians. We can, however, draw some conclusions about the gospel message from the way it arranges its material about Jesus.

Almost all of the miracles are set in the first part, leading up to the disciples' acknowledgement of Jesus as the Messiah. Until then Jesus' miracles outweigh the teaching, yet he does not perform miracles in order to prove to the crowds that he is the Messiah. Quite the opposite; again and again he tells the healed people and their friends not to tell anyone how they were healed.

Jesus was determined to be accepted on his own terms, not as someone fulfilling the popular, nationalistic expectations of what the Messiah would do for his people. He would accept the title 'Son of David', but not the fantasy of winning political freedom for the Jews of Palestine, restoring King David's little Hebrew empire and dominating the neighbouring nations. Whenever people tried to make him a king he refused.

Jesus consistently waited for a free response from people and never forced himself on them. He only met people's needs when they brought them to him; and he taught mainly in parables, which required the listeners to think and to see their beliefs from his point of view. As in the Parable of the Sower, if they would not listen and believe in the way he wanted them to, he would do nothing to make them change their minds.

This even applied to his closest disciples. Not until he judged the time to be right did Jesus ask the disciples who they thought he was. By that time they had been with him for some two years and had seen what powers he had and how he used them. But like the rest, they must draw their own conclusions. Peter summed up their beliefs about him by telling Jesus that they believed he was the Messiah; Jesus ordered them strictly not to tell anyone (Mk 8:29-30). That affirmation of belief was confirmed by the transfiguration of Jesus before the eyes of three of them, Peter, James and John (Mk 9:2-8), and Jesus then began his last journey towards Jerusalem.

The disciples still had much to learn, but Jesus could now begin to teach them in earnest, particularly about the way he would finally demonstrate his understanding of Messiah in the crucifixion and resurrection.

There are only two more miracles in Mark's Gospel. One is the healing of blind Bartimaeus just before Jesus entered Jerusalem in triumph. The other is the cursing and withering of the unfruitful fig tree, a miracle whose two stages are set by Mark either side of Jesus driving the traders from the temple.

The message is simple. Only those who are prepared to have faith in Jesus can have their blindness healed and see who he really is. The Hebrew people and their leaders, specially prepared by God to recognise the Messiah when he came, failed to welcome him when he finally entered Jerusalem. Some thought that Jesus was a threat to their authority, some thought that he should use his powers to bring political freedom, and some could not fit Jesus into their ideas about God.

THE MIRACLES IN LUKE'S GOSPEL

The gospel as a sequence of journeys

Unlike the other gospels, the author of Luke's Gospel continues the account of the origins of Christianity far on into the years that followed the ascension of Jesus. This sequel to Luke's Gospel – the Acts of the Apostles – shows how Jesus' disciples continued his work. Both the gospel and Acts have a similar literary structure, a continuous sequence of journeys. These journeys take Jesus from his conception in Nazareth to his death, resurrection and ascension in Jerusalem, and then show how the gospel of Jesus spread from Jerusalem out into the Roman empire.

The journeys in Luke's Gospel and Acts are more than mere travel information, they are the structure which supports the narrative. They draw attention to the pattern running through the details of the story: the explosive effects of God's power as it transformed the old Jewish beliefs and expanded into the new, Greek-speaking world where Luke's readers lived. Luke's literary structure is his main way of emphasising the invincible progress of God's plans.

To Luke's readers in the Greek-speaking towns of the eastern Mediterranean where Paul had stayed on his mission journeys, this structure would link them geographically and spiritually with the origins of Christianity in Palestinian Judaism. The journeys would show how the gospel had reached them as the New Israel expanded from Palestine to 'the ends of the earth', and from Jerusalem to Rome, the city at the centre of the empire. Coupled with the journeys, Luke's repeated references to the Holy Spirit would also demonstrate to them that they too shared fully in the power which moved Jesus himself, and which he had poured out on his apostles.

The journeys

The places which are linked by the journeys in Luke's Gospel are real places, but they take on a special significance as symbols of the new ways in which God has been working in his world since the birth of Jesus.

Luke's gospel starts with two such locations which are both real and symbolic: Jerusalem and Nazareth. Jerusalem was the centre of international Judaism in a world where far more Jews lived outside Palestine than within it. The city contained the temple, the place of God's presence and the only place in the world where Judaism officially permitted Jews to offer the sacrifices required by their religion. It was also the city of King David, the national hero and model for the Messiah, who had united the warring Hebrew tribes, defeated all the other national groups in Palestine, and established the Hebrew national state.

If Jerusalem was the symbol of ancient Jewish privileges and hopes, Nazareth was its antithesis. Unmentioned in the Old Testament, Nazareth was an insignificant town in Galilee, a region of Palestine notorious for its mixture of races. Two great international routes merged and crossed in Galilee, carrying invaders, migrants and traders, each of whom made their contribution to the variety of settlers. The Jews of Jerusalem contemptuously referred to it as the 'district of the Gentiles', the 'foreigners'. But as more and more Gentiles from the many races of the Roman empire were attracted to Christianity, Nazareth took on a new significance as the place where Jesus himself was conceived, and where he spent the major part of his life. Nazareth was the place where the exclusive Jewish mould of the Old Covenant was broken for ever.

Luke's journey sequence begins with Mary, pregnant with Jesus, travelling from Nazareth to Judah, the traditional Jewish heart-land, to visit her cousin Elizabeth, pregnant with John the Baptist. John is destined to be the herald of Jesus the Messiah. In the next journey, Mary and Joseph travel from Nazareth to Bethlehem, just south of Jerusalem, David's birthplace and the ancestral centre of the tribe of Judah, and Jesus was born while they were there.

From Bethlehem, the journey continues to the Temple in Jerusalem, so that Joseph and Mary may offer the minor sacrifice prescribed by the Jewish ritual law after childbirth. There, at the most sacred place on earth for Jews, Simeon proclaimed Jesus as the saviour of both Gentiles and Jews, in words familiar to Jews from the prophet Isaiah. The narrative returns the family to the obscurity of Nazareth, to end a journey in which Luke had drawn together all the main features of Jewish hopes, even the extension of the ancient covenant to include all peoples.

The next journey occurs when Jesus reached the age of twelve and goes with his family to Jerusalem for the feast of Passover and Unleavened Bread. Luke makes the main point about this journey through his first recorded words of Jesus: 'Did you not know that I must be in my Father's house?' (Lk 2:49).

The final journey in Luke's Gospel begins at 9:51, after the baptism, temptations and Galilean ministry of Jesus, and occupies nearly ten chapters. Luke provides the essential clue to this journey's significance at the beginning of it: '...as the days drew near for him to be received up, he set his face to go to Jerusalem' (Lk 9:51). In that phrase, the crucifixion, resurrection and ascension are combined into one event, and everything which happens during the journey is a comment about it. So what appear to be comparatively mundane incidents take on a new significance. This final journey is packed with descriptions of encounters, teaching, parables and miracles. Every incident in it is a comment on the kind of life which Christians should follow as a consequence of the death, resurrection and ascension of their Lord, Jesus the Christ.

The journeys begin again in the Acts of the Apostles, Luke's sequel to his gospel, but now it is the apostles who are travelling. Their journeys show the expansion of Christianity, first within Palestine and then beyond it into the Gentile world, until the final journey reaches Rome, the centre of the world, where the new faith has already taken root. The risen Jesus is presented by Luke as the new focus for the world's hope and the saviour of all peoples, with the Roman empire as the symbol of God's universal rule.

The miracles in Luke's Gospel

Title	Type	Matthew	Mark	Luke	John
The man in the synagogue in Capernaum	E		1:23-28	**4:33-37**	
Peter's mother-in-law	H	8:14-15	1:29-31	**4:38-39**	
A great catch of fish	N			**5:4-10**	
A leper	H&P	8:1-4	1:40-45	**5:12-16**	
A paralysed man in Capernaum	H	9:1-8	2:1-12	**5:17-26**	
A man with a withered hand	H	12:9-14	3:1-6	**6:6-11**	
The centurion's servant	H	8:5-13		**7:1-10**	
A widow's son at Nain	R			**7:11-17**	
(Mary Magdalene	E		16:9	**8:2**)	
The storm stilled	N	8:23-27	4:35-41	**8:22-25**	
The man of Gerasa	D	8:28-34	5:1-20	**8:26-39**	
Jairus' daughter	R	9:18-26	5:21-43	**8:40-56**	
The woman with an issue of blood	H&P	9:20-22	5:23-34	**8:43-48**	
Feeding the 5000	N	14:13-21	6:30-44	**9:10-17**	6:1-14
The epileptic boy	E	17:14-17	9:14-21	**9:37-43**	
A dumb man	E	9:32-33		**11:14**	
The woman bent double in a synagogue	E			**13:10-17**	
A dropsical man	H			**14:1-6**	
Ten lepers	H&P			**17:11-19**	
Blind Bartimaeus	H	20:29-34	10:46-52	**18:35-43**	
The high priest's servant	H			**22:50-51**	

Key: E: Exorcism; H: Healing; N: Nature; P: Purification; R: Resurrection.

Luke's Gospel records twenty-one miracles, of which only five are set in the narrative – more than nine chapters long – of Jesus' final journey to Jerusalem. The final miracle, recorded only by Luke, is the healing of the man whose ear was cut off by one of the disciples during the arrest of Jesus in the Garden of Gethsemane.

All the journeys in Luke symbolise the presence of God's invincible power, but Luke's Gospel proclaims the messianic identity of Jesus in the first public words of Jesus it records. Appropriately, the occasion was a sabbath in Jesus' home town, Nazareth, and it occurred in the synagogue he normally attended.

Surrounded by people who knew him well, Jesus selected a well known messianic passage from the Book of the Prophet Isaiah and read it out:

'The Spirit of the Lord is upon me,
because he has anointed me
to preach good news to the poor.
He has sent me to proclaim release to the captives
and recovery of sight to the blind,
to set at liberty those who are oppressed,
to proclaim the acceptable year of the Lord'
(Lk 4:18-19).

Then Jesus told the congregation that this prophetic passage had been fulfilled as they were listening to him. Jesus' townsfolk were impressed by his eloquence but scandalised by his claims for himself, and when Jesus rebuked them for their unbelief they tried to kill him.

Luke's Gospel immediately begins to record miracles as evidence that Jesus' claims were true. Some of these miracles are also recorded in Mark and Matthew, and some are only recorded again in Matthew. Six of the miracles are only found in Luke's Gospel itself. Clearly, Luke selected carefully from all the available material in order to meet the needs of his own readership and to support the particular emphasis of his gospel.

Luke's special emphasis on Jesus' compassion for the poor and rejected is evident in the miracles Luke alone records: the resurrection of the widow's son at Nain, the woman bent double in a synagogue, the dropsical man and the ten lepers. But these also point to the narrow-mindedness of the Jewish religious authorities, and one of them emphasises the special gratitude and faith of a Samaritan leper in contrast with the Jewish ones. Luke was writing especially Christian converts from the non-Jewish world. Only Luke records Jesus healing his enemy's injured servant during his arrest in the Garden of Gethsemane.

Another miracle unique to Luke, the great catch of fish, shows Jesus sharing his responsibilities and his powers with the disciples from the time he first called them. This is confirmed when Jesus sent them out in pairs throughout Galilee. They returned to report their success to Jesus, and to tell him that they could even exorcise demons in his name. Jesus told them that Satan had been defeated, and that nothing could prevent the eventual success of their missionary work. Luke would continue this theme in his companion work, the Acts of the Apostles, with its record of the success of the apostles far beyond Palestine and in Rome itself. That success was similarly marked by the miracles the apostles were able to do in the name of the risen Jesus.

The records of miracles Luke shares with other gospels serve the same theme, for the other gospels also bring out the particular concern Jesus had for the deprived and outcast. Like the other gospels, Luke indicates the range of Jesus' powers, and like them they all serve as signs pointing forward to the real significance of the crucifixion and resurrection. Jesus himself, in his own person, is the means of salvation, as stated in the apostles' preaching reported in Acts. The power Jesus shows in the miracles, and the way he uses it, is only a foretaste of the power which God demonstrated in Jesus' death and resurrection, and which is shared by all who turn to him.

THE MIRACLES IN JOHN'S GOSPEL

John's Gospel has a very different design and style from the other three, and there it has far less material in common with them than they have with each other. Although parts of it read like the vivid reports of eye-witnesses, particularly some of the extended conversations and controversies, other parts are carefully constructed theological reflections about Jesus. Many people believe that this gospel is the last of the four to be written or edited into the form we now have, perhaps as long as sixty years after the death of Jesus, and that it expresses the fruit of a long lifetime's reflection on the words and deeds of Jesus by one of the closest of his disciples. The seven miracles recorded in John before the crucifixion and resurrection of Jesus are vital elements in this gospel's structure.

The structure of John's Gospel and the miracles ('signs')

PROLOGUE (1:1-18)

JESUS MINISTRY (1:19 - 12:50)

The opening week in Judea and Galilee (1:19 - 2:12)
    The witness of John; the first disciples
        First sign: Water changed to wine
            (For the meaning of 'sign' see 20:30f)

The passover in Jerusalem (2:13 - 4:54)
    The cleansing of the temple
    The discourse with Nicodemus on baptism
    Jesus among the Samaritans
    Jesus back in Galilee
        Second sign: the cure of an official's son

The second feast at Jerusalem (5:1-47)
    Third sign: cure at the pool of Bethesda
    The discourse on judgement

The passover of the bread of life (6:1-71)
    Fourth sign: the feeding of the 5000
    Fifth sign: Jesus walks on water
    The discourse on the eucharist
    Peter's profession of faith

The Feast of tabernacles in Jerusalem (7:1 - 10:21)
    Arguments about the Messiah's origins
    The promise of living water
    Jesus the light of the world
    Argument about Jesus testifying to himself
    Sixth sign: the cure of the man born blind
    The good shepherd discourse

The feast of dedication in Jerusalem (10:22-42)
    Jesus claims to be Son of God
    Jesus withdraws beyond the Jordan

Jesus moves towards his death (11:1 -12:50)
    Seventh sign: the raising of Lazarus
    The Messiah enters Jerusalem
    The unbelief of the Jews

JESUS' HOUR COMES (13:1 - 20:31)

Jesus' last meal with his disciples (13:1 - 17:26)
    The washing of feet
    Farewell discourses
    The prayer of Jesus

The passion (18:1 - 19:42)
    The arrest

Before Annas and Caiaphas; Peter's denials
Before Pilate
The crucifixion
The burial

The day of resurrection (20:1-30)
The empty tomb
Jesus appears to Mary of Magdala
Appearances of Jesus to the disciples
The purpose of the signs (20:30-31)

EPILOGUE (21:1-25)

Jesus appears at the Sea of Galilee
Second conclusion

John's structure and Hebrew festivals

Unlike the other three gospels, John shows Jesus in Jerusalem several times during his ministry, at Hebrew festivals. The major festivals were central to the Hebrew religion, and the prescribed sacrifices could only be offered in Jerusalem itself. For John, the festivals show Jesus fulfilling these central obligations of the old religion and replacing them by himself:

2:13	Passover (relates to 1:19 - 4:54)
5:1	An unnamed festival (relates to 5:1-47)
6:4	Passover (relates to 6:1-71)
7:2	Tabernacles (relates to 7:1 - 10:21)
10:22	Dedication of the temple (relates to 10:22-54)
11:55	Passover (relates to 11:1 - 12:50; 13:1 - 20:31)

The miracles ('signs') in John's Gospel

Title	Type	Matthew	Mark	Luke	John
Water changed to wine	N				2:1-11
The son of an official at Capernaum	H				4:46-54
A paralysed man, pool of Bethesda	H				5:1-9
Feeding the 5000	N	14:13-21	6:30-44	9:10-17	6:1-14
Walking on water	N	14:22-33	6:45-52		6:16-21
A blind man born blind	H				9:1-7
The raising of Lazarus	R				11:1-44
A catch of fish	N				21:6-11

Key: H: Healings; N: Nature; R: Resurrection.

The twelve chapters of John's Gospel which deal with Jesus' ministry (1:19 - 12:50) are called ' The Book of Signs' by some commentators, because they contain seven of the eight miracles recorded in this gospel, and John refers to them as ' signs'. The gospel also explains why these have been selected:

'Now Jesus did many other signs in the presence of the disciples, which are not written in this book; but these are written that you may believe that Jesus is the Christ, the Son of God, and that believing you may have life in his name' (Jn 20:30-31).

Whoever John's Gospel was written for, possibly a Christian community in Asia Minor, these seven miracles were selected to help them understand who Jesus was and what he could do for them. The eighth miracle, the catch of fish (Jn 21:6-11) is part of the final commissioning of the disciples before Jesus leaves them for the last time.

John's Gospel starts by explaining that Jesus is the creative word of God through whom everything came into existence; he is also the invincible and inextinguishable light of God by which everyone can find God and be united with him; this ultimate, personal, creative and saving power 'became flesh', suffered, died and rose from the dead 'that all who believe in him should not perish but have eternal life' (Jn 3:16). The miracles are signs which help to explain what all this means, assisted by the discourses which John's Gospel associates with them.

The water turned to wine at the wedding feast (2:1-11), signifies the transformation of the Jewish rituals of purification by Jesus. As he explained to Nicodemus, during the Passover festival which immediately follows, it is necessary to be born again of water and the spirit in order to enter the kingdom of God.

The second sign is the healing of the official's son who is near death at Capernaum (4:46-54); this leads to the man and his whole household committing themselves to Jesus. It is followed immediately by the third sign, the healing of the paralysed man at the Pool of Bethesda in Jerusalem (5:1-9). In sharp contrast to the conversion of the Jewish official and his household, this miracle leads to a fierce controversy with the Jewish religious authorities for breach of the sabbath. These two signs are then linked with the discourse on Jesus as judge and as the source of life. Judgement comes from rejecting Jesus and his saving power; life comes from accepting Jesus and turning from sin (Jn 5:14).

The fourth sign, the feeding of the 5000 (Jn 6:1-14), and the fifth, walking on water (Jn 6:16-21), both occur in other gospels. But John links them with the discourse on the eucharist and Jesus as the bread of life. Once more, the claims made by Jesus are stupendous, to the point where everyone except the twelve disciples leaves him.

The sixth sign, the healing of the man born blind (Jn 9:1-7), precipitates a controversy between the man and the religious authorities, who are convinced that Jesus is a sinner. They try unsuccessfully to get the man to agree with them. When Jesus returns to the man he acknowledges Jesus as the

Messiah and worships him. This belief theme passes naturally into one of judgement when Jesus tells him that it is those who think they can see, such as the Jewish religious leaders, who are really blind. The incident is followed by the discourse on Jesus as the good shepherd who lays down his life for his sheep.

Finally, the seventh sign, the raising of Lazarus from the dead (Jn 11:1-44), is accompanied by Jesus' claim that he himself is the resurrection and the life, and that whoever believes in him will never die. It is a fitting climax to the signs as Jesus moves forward to his own death and resurrection.

The signs interact further with the series of festivals which Jesus attends at the temple in Jerusalem. These consist of three Passovers, an unnamed festival and the Feast of Dedication. The temple was the unique centre of Jewish religion, where God was most surely to be found, and the only place on earth where Jews could legally take part in the sacrificial ritual of their religion.

The Dedication commemorated the purification of the temple after it had been defiled by pagan worship. The Passovers commemorated the exodus from Egypt, the great redemptive event which gave reality to the covenant between God and his people.

Together with the miracles, Jesus' involvement in these festivals at the temple point forward to his own final Passover, when he established the decisive redemptive event for Christians by passing through death to eternal life. All who believed in him as Son of God would be able to relate fully to God through the risen Jesus, the new temple.

The four gospels and the miracles

Each in its own way, the four gospels select and arrange the miracles to bring out the significance of Jesus. He is not a mere teacher who provides his audiences – and particularly his disciples – with a new system of religious belief, or a new code of religious law, or even a new set of ideals. Nor is he merely a supreme example of how to live a life of full response to God's love. If he were no more than teacher or example he would leave his followers frustrated by their inability to put his teaching into practice or to follow his example.

The gospels present Jesus as the power and love of God come in human form. The miracles help to indicate the full range of that power and love, which Jesus demonstrated most completely not in his miracles but in his death and resurrection.

This could still be no more than a frustrating event impossible to imitate. But the first Christians, for whom the four gospels were written, believed that they could share in the person of the risen Jesus and in the power of the Spirit by which he lived. They believed that this sharing was intimately associated with baptism and the eucharist, and that nothing on earth – or anywhere else – could separate them from the love of God made manifest in Jesus. The miracles were selected and recorded to help them to appreciate the full range of this love and its power to transform their lives.

10

The miracles and the significance of Jesus

In the Roman world, crucifixions were the normal way of executing condemned criminals who had no special social status; privileged classes were beheaded or allowed to commit suicide. It was inevitable that Jesus would be condemned to crucifixion once Pontius Pilate had accepted that he was guilty of the treason charge levelled against him in the Roman court by the Jewish leaders. Passers-by would have observed nothing unusual about the crucifixion of Jesus. The only difference between this crucifixion and all the countless other ones turned on the identity of Jesus, the central of the three condemned men being crucified that day outside the walls of Jerusalem.

All of the gospel material is dedicated to demonstrating and supporting that difference, and the miracles are a vital part of that material. Like everything else in the gospels, the background to the miracles is the pattern of beliefs preached by the apostles: who Jesus is, what he achieved, how he achieved it, and what his status is now. This is what the stories of the miracles meant for the first Christians, who responded to the apostles' invitation to repent, accept Jesus as their risen Lord, and be baptised. Within each gospel, the miracles help to direct the reader towards the crucifixion, resurrection and ascension of Jesus, and to explain what was really happening in those decisive events.

The nature miracles signify that the person being crucified was far more than a Jewish idealist and faith-healer. He was the divine agent of creation. Through him the universe had been made; it was still being sustained through him, and through him it would be brought to its ultimate consummation. He had calmed the storm and walked on the waters, just as the first account of creation in Genesis depicted God imposing order on the primeval chaos. That same creative power had redeemed the Hebrew people from their slavery in Egypt and led them through the waters to the freedom and order of the covenant. So too, the crucifixion was a new and far more decisive journey through death, so that all could share in the new life of the risen Jesus and the freedom of the new covenant. This new life of union with God could be celebrated within the Christian communities by means of the eucharist, 'the Lord's Supper' instituted by Jesus on the night before the crucifixion, and prefigured in his miraculous feeding of the hungry crowds who had followed him.

The crucifixion was the climax of the enmity Jesus had aroused in the Jewish civil and religious authorities during his public ministry. But it was far more than this for the apostles and first Christians. It was the supreme effort of the powers of personal evil to win the decisive victory in their war against God. The miracles of exorcism show Jesus defeating evil of every kind, whether it appeared in solitary or multiple form, whether in Jesus' presence or at a distance, whether in Jewish or Gentile territory. The apostles and first Christians believed that Jesus finally subjected himself to the full force of evil by allowing himself to be crucified, and that his resurrection demonstrated that God's power was superior to anything that evil could do.

Execution by crucifixion was the ultimate defilement in Hebrew law which rendered the victim totally outcast. It had to be performed beyond the walls lest it defile the whole city; no part of the long process could take place during a religious festival or the festival itself would be defiled. Jesus had overcome lesser defilements in people by miracles of purification, such as the healing of lepers and of the woman with an issue of blood. Now he himself submitted to this ultimate defilement, and demonstrated in his own person that the power of God's holiness could cleanse even this.

In a whole range of miracles Jesus had brought people back to life again, and had restored their impaired bodily faculties to full health. Now in his own body, he not only submitted to death, but to a form of execution which slowly, deliberately and systematically destroyed the victim's bodily faculties. The gospels emphasise that the body of the risen Jesus was the same body that was executed, bearing the wounds of crucifixion and the final thrust of the soldier's spear. Jesus demonstrated that his risen life was a restoration of the whole person with the full range of human faculties, not just the survival past death of 'reason' or even of 'soul' or 'spirit'.

The practicalities of belief

Whatever else they might be, the beliefs of the first Christians about Jesus were essentially practical beliefs with practical applications. Far from holding merely abstract or theoretical beliefs, the Christians used their beliefs to apply the power of the risen Jesus to their everyday lives. Baptism, they believed, initiated each of them into an intimate personal union with the risen Jesus, which gave them a share in his new life and in the powers he had demonstrated during his ministry and in his own death and resurrection. This belief is amply demonstrated in the New Testament letters, which open windows on to the lives of the first Christians and the matters which caused them concern.

They believed that their world was subject to a whole range of spiritual forces, good as well as evil. Some of the popular religions they had left gave expression to these beliefs. Their Christianity gave them the confidence that whatever powers there might be – in heaven, on earth or in the underworld of their three-decker universe, they were all created by God and subordinate to him. As sharers in the sonship of Christ, they believed that they were no longer at the mercy of such forces:

> '...we are more than conquerors through him who loved us. For I am sure that neither death, nor life, nor angels, nor principalities, nor things present, nor things to come, nor powers... nor anything else in all creation, will be able to separate us from the love of God in Christ Jesus our Lord' (Rom 8:37-39).

As they shared in the very power which brought the universe into existence and sustained it, they could not be harmed by anything in it.

Equally, Jesus had transcended all the criteria by which the world judged some people to be inferior to others and excluded them from their society, whether race, family, education, profession, religious inheritance, or anything else. He had demonstrated this in the miracles of purification, and in his own surmounting of the defilement of crucifixion. The risen Jesus was the beginning of a new society in which no one was outcast, a new people of God, composed of all who are united to him.

In that new community there is no place for the distinctions which dominant groups use to allocate status, such as Jew and Gentile, slave and free, barbarian and civilised, or even male and female; for 'Christ is all, and in all' (Col 3:11). If no one in this society is inferior to another, neither is anyone superior to any other; so 'put on then, as God's chosen ones, holy and beloved, compassion, kindness, meekness, and patience, forbearing one another...' (Col 3:12). The ideals set out by Jesus in the Sermon on the Mount are the standards of the all-inclusive community of the risen Jesus. The miracles demonstrate that the power is available to put the ideals into practice.

The members of the new community of the risen Jesus are also able to overcome whatever might hinder them from expressing their full humanity towards each other. In his miracles of healing Jesus had restored the damaged limbs, eyes, ears, tongues and hands of all who were brought to him. He had suffered similar destruction of his own human faculties in his crucified body, and in the same risen body he had demonstrated their indestructible restoration. The members of the new community, the body of the risen Jesus, share his power and can overcome whatever hinders them from using their human faculties in his service and in the service of each other.

The miracles and suffering

If it is feared that such beliefs might encourage complacency in the first Christians, it would be quickly dispelled by their experience of suffering and the way their apostolic teachers related this experience to the sufferings of Jesus.

The gospels record that during the crucifixion Jesus was taunted with the challenge to save himself miraculously from his suffering: '...the rulers scoffed at him, saying, He saved others; let him save himself, if he is the Christ of God, his Chosen One!' (Lk 23:35). But Jesus chose to suffer and die; and by his obedience to the point of death and beyond, he made redemption available for all.

In a number of places the New Testament letters observe that their union with the risen Christ does not protect Christians from suffering. On the contrary, their sufferings are positive evidence of that union. The most thorough treatment of this is to be found in Paul's Second Letter to the Corinthians.

Immediately after the brief greetings with which the letter opens, Paul plunges straight into an analysis of what the Christian can discover from suffering. The experience of suffering, he says, makes it easier to help others with their suffering, because along with the suffering comes also the realisation that God gives the power to cope with it. This then confirms the Christians' belief that all their suffering is a sharing in Christ's sufferings, and the power to cope with it is evidence that they are also sharing in the help Christ received from God.

Moreover, Paul continues, sharing in Christ's sufferings contributes to the help, and even to the salvation, received by others. Consequently, they in their turn gain access to the power of God, the 'comfort, which you experience when you patiently endure the same sufferings that we suffer' (2 Cor 1:6).

***

The four gospels are only selections from the information that was available about Jesus at the time when they were compiled, and the miracles are only a part of those selections. They are an important part, but if they are studied in isolation from the rest of the material they can lead to seriously distorted beliefs about Jesus and about the kind of salvation he achieved for humankind. In particular, the miracles must be related to the parables of Jesus, and not only to the contents of the parables but to the beliefs about faith and personal responsibility such a method of teaching implies.

Jesus was not a mere miracle-worker, not even the most spectacular miracle-worker ever known. For Christians, he was the Son of God incarnate, the redeemer of the world and the eternal hope of all who believe in him. The miracles are not the only evidence for these beliefs about Jesus, but they are powerful signs of what such beliefs actually mean.

Index of miracles in the four gospels

Key to miracle type: E: Exorcism; H: Healing; N: Nature;
P: Purification; R: Resurrection.

Miracle	Type	Matthew	Mark	Luke	John
Exorcisms					
A blind and dumb man	E	12:22			
The Canaanite woman's daughter	E	15:21-28	7:24-30		
A dumb man	E	9:32-33		11:14	
The epileptic boy	E	17:14-17	9:14-21	9:37-43	
The man or men of Gerasa (Gerasene swine)	E	8:28-34	5:1-20	8:26-39	
The man in the synagogue in Capernaum	E		1:23-28	4:33-37	
(Mary Magdalene	E		16:9	8:2)	
The woman bent double in a synagogue	E			13:10-17	
Healings with no mention of demons					
Blind Bartimaeus	H	20:29-34	10:46-52	18:35-43	
A blind man at Bethsaida	H		8:22-26		
A blind man born blind	H				9:1-7
Two blind men	H	9:27-31			
The centurion's servant	H	8:5-13		7:1-10	

141

Miracle	Type	Matthew	Mark	Luke	John
A deaf mute	H		7:31-37		
A dropsical man	H			14:1-6	
A leper	H&P	8:1-4	1:40-45	5:12-16	
Ten lepers	H&P			17:11-19	
A paralysed man in Capernaum	H	9:1-8	2:1-12	5:17-26	
A paralysed man at the Pool of Bethesda	H				5:1-9
Peter's mother-in-law	H	8:14-15	1:29-31	4:38-39	
The high priest's slave	H			22:50-51	
The son of an official at Capernaum	H				4:46-54
A man with a withered hand	H	12:9-14	3:1-6	6:6-11	
The woman with an issue of blood	H&P	9:20-22	5:23-34	8:43-48	

Raising the dead

Miracle	Type	Matthew	Mark	Luke	John
Jairus' daughter	R	9:18-26	5:21-43	8:40-56	
Lazarus	R				11:1-44
The son of a widow at Nain	R			7:11-17	

Nature miracles

Miracle	Type	Matthew	Mark	Luke	John
The great catch of fish	N			5:4-10	
Another catch of fish	N				21:6-11
The Coin in a fish's mouth	N	17:24-27			
Feeding the 5000	N	14:13-21	6:30-44	9:10-17	6:1-14
Feeding the 4000	N	15:32-39	8:1-10		
A fig tree cursed	N	21:18-22	11:12-14, 20-24		
The storm stilled	N	8:23-27	4:35-41	8:22-25	
Walking on water	N	14:22-33	6:45-52		6:16-21
Water changed to wine	N				2:1-11

Miracle	Type	Matthew	Mark	Luke	John

Matthew's miracles

Miracle	Type	Matthew	Mark	Luke	John
A leper	H&P	**8:1-4**	1:40-45	5:12-16	
The centurion's servant	H	**8:5-13**	7:1-10		
Peter's mother-in-law	H	**8:14-15**	1:29-31	4:38-39	
The storm stilled	N	**8:23-27**	4:35-41	8:22-25	
The man or men of Gerasa	E	**8:28-34**	5:1-20	8:26-39	
A paralysed man in Capernaum	H	**9:1-8**	2:1-12	5:17-26	
Jairus' daughter	R	**9:18-26**	5:21-43	8:40-56	
The woman with an issue of blood	H&P	**9:20-22**	5:23-34	8:43-48	
Two blind men	H	**9:27-31**			
A dumb man	E	**9:32-33**		11:14	
A man with a withered hand	H	**12:9-14**	3:1-6	6:6-11	
A blind and dumb man	E	**12:22**			
Feeding the 5000	N	**14:13-21**	6:30-44	9:10-17	6:1-14
Walking on water	N	**14:22-33**	6:45-52		6:16-21
The Canaanite woman's daughter	E	**15:21-28**	7:24-30		
Feeding the 4000	N	**15:32-39**	8:1-10		
The epileptic boy	E	**17:14-17**	9:14-21	9:37-43	
The coin in a fish's mouth	N	**17:24-27**			
Blind Bartimaeus	H	**20:29-34**	10:46-52	18:35-43	
A fig tree cursed	N	**21:18-22**	11:12-14, 20-24		

Mark's miracles

Miracle	Type	Matthew	Mark	Luke	John
A man in the synagogue in Capernaum	E		**1:23-28**	4:33-37	
Peter's mother-in-law	H	8:14-15	**1:29-31**	4:38-39	
A leper	H&P	8:1-4	**1:40-45**	5:12-16	
A paralysed man in Capernaum	H	9:1-8	**2:1-12**	5:17-26	
A man with a withered hand	H	12:9-14	**3:1-6**	6:6-11	

143

Miracle	Type	Matthew	Mark	Luke	John
The storm stilled	N	8:23-27	**4:35-41**	8:22-25	
The man or men of Gerasa	E	8:28-34	**5:1-20**	8:26-39	
Jairus' daughter	R	9:18-26	**5:21-43**	8:40-56	
The woman with an issue of blood	H&P	9:20-22	**5:23-34**	8:43-48	
Feeding the 5000	N	14:13-21	**6:30-44**	9:10-17	6:1-14
Walking on water	N	14:22-33	**6:45-52**		6:16-21
The centurion's servant	H	8:5-13	**7:1-10**		
The Canaanite woman's daughter	E	15:21-28	**7:24-30**		
A deaf mute	H		**7:31-37**		
Feeding the 4000	N	15:32-39	**8:1-10**		
A blind man at Bethsaida	H		**8:22-26**		
The epileptic boy	E	17:14-17	**9:14-21**	9:37-43	
Blind Bartimaeus	H	20:29-34	**10:46-52**	18:35-43	
A fig tree cursed	N	21:18-22	**11:12-14, 20-24**		
(Mary Magdalene	E		**16:9**	8:2)	

Luke's miracles

Miracle	Type	Matthew	Mark	Luke	John
A man in the synagogue in Capernaum	E		1:23-28	**4:33-37**	
Peter's mother-in-law	H	8:14-15	1:29-31	**4:38-39**	
A great catch of fish	N			**5:4-10**	
A leper	H&P	8:1-4	1:40-45	**5:12-16**	
A paralysed man in Capernaum	H	9:1-8	2:1-12	**5:17-26**	
A man with a withered hand	H	2:9-14	3:1-6	**6:6-11**	
The centurion's servant	H	8:5-13		**7:1-10**	
A widow's son at Nain	R			**7:11-17**	
(Mary Magdalene	E		16:9	**8:2)**	
The storm stilled	N	8:23-27	4:35-41	**8:22-25**	
The man or men of Gerasa	E	8:28-34	5:1-20	**8:26-39**	
Jairus' daughter	R	9:18-26	5:21-43	**8:40-56**	

144

Miracle	Type	Matthew	Mark	Luke	John
The woman with an issue of blood	H&P	9:20-22	5:23-34	**8:43-48**	
Feeding the 5000	N	14:13-21	6:30-44	**9:10-17**	6:1-14
The epileptic boy	E	17:14-17	9:14-21	**9:37-43**	
A dumb man	E	9:32-33		**11:14**	
The woman bent double in a synagogue	E			**13:10-17**	
A dropsical man	H			**14:1-6**	
The lepers	H			**17:11-19**	
Blind Bartimaeus	H	20:29-34	10:46-52	**18:35-43**	
The high priest's slave	H			**22:50-51**	

John's miracles

	Type	Matthew	Mark	Luke	John
Water changed to wine	N				**2:1-11**
The son of an official at Capernaum	H				**4:46-54**
A paralysed man at the Pool of Bethesda	H				**5:1-9**
Feeding the 5000	N	14:13-21	6:30-44	9:10-17	**6:1-14**
Walking on water	N	14:22-33	6:45-52		**6:16-21**
A blind man born blind	H				**9:1-7**
Lazarus	R				**11:1-44**
A catch of fish	N				**21:6-11**

The Miracles
and the Liturgy

THE ROMAN CATHOLIC LITURGY

Sunday	*Title of Miracle*	*Page*
Cycle A		
Lent 4	A blind man born blind	63
Lent 5	The raising of Lazarus	53
18th Sunday	The feeding of 5000	36
19th Sunday	Walking on water	39
20th Sunday	The Canaanite woman's daughter	99
Cycle B		
4th Sunday	The man in a synagogue in Capernaum	96
6th Sunday	A leper	84
7th Sunday	A paralysed man in Capernaum	73
9th Sunday	A man with a withered hand	75
12th Sunday	The storm stilled	35
13th Sunday	The raising of Jairus' daughter	51
	The woman with an issue of blood	86
17th Sunday	The feeding of 5000	36
23rd Sunday	A deaf-mute	79
30th Sunday	Blind Bartimaeus	66
Cycle C		
Easter 3	A catch of fish	33
Corpus Christ	The feeding of 5000	36
2nd Sunday	Water changed to wine	31

Sunday	Title of Miracle	Page
5th Sunday	A great catch of fish	44
9th Sunday	The centurion's servant	70
10th Sunday	The raising of a widow's son at Nain	50
28th Sunday	Ten lepers	91

THE CHURCH OF ENGLAND LITURGY

1. The Book of Common Prayer

Sunday	Title of Miracle	Page
Epiphany 4	The storm stilled	35
	The men of Gerasa	98
Lent 2	The Canaanite woman's daughter	99
Lent 3	A dumb man	103
Lent 4	Feeding the 5000	36
Trinity 7	Feeding the 4000	40
Trinity 12	A deaf-mute	79
Trinity 14	Ten lepers	91
Trinity 16	The raising of a widow's son at Nain	50
Trinity 17	A dropsical man	90
Trinity 19	A paralysed man in Capernaum	73
Trinity 21	The son of an official at Capernaum	88
Trinity 24	The raising of Jairus' daughter	51
	The woman with an issue of blood	86
Trinity 25	Feeding the 5000	36

2. The Alternative Service Book 1980

Year 1

Epiphany 3	Water changed to wine	31
8th b. Easter	A paralysed man in Capernaum	73
Thursday in Easter Week	A catch of fish	33
Easter 3	A catch of fish	33
17th a. Pent.	Ten lepers	91

Sunday	*Title of Miracle*	*Page*
Year 2		
Epiphany 3	Feeding the 5000	36
8th b. Easter	The Canaanite woman's daughter	99
Lent 2	A blind and dumb man	103
Easter 3	The raising of Lazarus	53
3rd a. Pent.	The raising of Jairus' daughter	51
	The woman with an issue of blood	86
6th a. Pent.	Blind Bartimaeus	66
9th a. Pent.	The epileptic boy	101
17th a. Pent.	The centurion's servant	70
21st a. Pent.	The raising of Lazarus	53

Suggestions
for further reading

All the biblical quotations in this book are taken, with permission, from the Revised Standard Version (RSV) of the Bible. This is a good translation, widely approved by most Christian Churches, including the Roman Catholic Church. Some other modern translations are easier to use because they divide the material into paragraphs and sections with headings. These include *The Catholic Study Bible*, *The New Jerusalem Bible* and *The Good News Bible*.

J. Rhymer, *The Bible in Order* (1975), presents the four gospels in a chronological order and their relationship to the rest of the biblical material.

There are a number of general commentaries on the Bible, which have good sections on the miracles of Jesus. These include:

New Bible Commentary, edited by G. Guthrie & others (3rd edition, 1970);
The New Jerome Commentary, edited by R.E. Brown & others (1989).

There are an enormous number of books on Jesus and the Gospels, including:

H. Conzelmann, *Jesus* (1973)

M. Cook, *The Jesus of Faith* (1981)

C.H. Dodd, *The Apostolic Preaching and its Developments* (1936)

C.H. Dodd, *The Founder of Christianity* (1971)

L. Goppelt, *The Theology of the New Testament 1: The Ministry of Jesus* (1981)

A.M. Hunter, *The Work and Words of Jesus* (1950)

J. Mackey, *Jesus the Man and the Myth* (1979)

N. Perrin, *Rediscovering the Teaching of Jesus* (1967)

V. Taylor, *The Gospels* (1960)

G. Vermes, *Jesus the Jew* (1973)

D. Watson, *Jesus Then and Now* (1983)

I. Wilson, *Jesus: the Evidence* (1984)

Books on miracles include:

A. Fridrichsen, *The Problem of Miracle in Primitive Christianity* (1972)

R.H. Fuller, *Interpreting the Miracles*, (1963)

H.C. Kee, *Miracle in the Early Christian World* (1983)

G. Mackrell, *The Healing Miracles in Mark's Gospel* (1987)

C.F.D. Moule (ed.), *Miracles* (1965)

F. Mussner, *The Miracles of Jesus* (1968)

H.J. Richards, *The Miracles of Jesus* (1975)

A. Richardson, *The Miracle Stories of the Gospels* (1941)

G. Theissen, *The Miracle Stories of the Early Christian Tradition* (1983)

H. Van der Loos, *The Miracles of Jesus* (1965)

THE HEALING MIRACLES IN MARK'S GOSPEL

Gerard Mackrell

Confronted by human misery we have the option of facing it and trying to make sense of it or of seeking refuge in a form of escapism that is worse than the evil from which one tries to escape. Mark's Gospel faces suffering at its most radical and hideous source – evil itself, Satan; in himself and in us. His Gospel also dwells on those particular manifestations of evil: the various diseases of mind and body and soul; and how Jesus healed to the roots of the being. But no anaesthetics in this healing. Mark, more than any other evangelist, is overshadowed by that Cross where the ultimate surgery, again unaesthetised, was 'performed'. And on Calvary he sees our fullest and deepest healing. Through his Passion, rather than through his healing miracles, did Jesus show his compassion. In the healing miracles described in this book we find Mark insisting: 'In the Cross the lasting healing of he who is forever "health and wholeness and sending" – through Jesus Christ'.

ISBN 085439 263 7   138 pp.   £4.95

JESUS THE HEALER

Andrew Myer

In the gospels we see Jesus engaged in a continuous fight against diseases of all kinds. He is as concerned about the fever of Peter's mother-in-law as he is about the plight of the paralytic or the man possessed by a crowd of demons. What strikes us most about the healing ministry of Jesus is that he always gives preference to the poor and the discriminated: women and children who have fewer rights, workers who are poorly paid, the untouchables of society like the lepers and the mentally ill.

However, before working a healing miracle Jesus invariably brings up the question of faith. Those in need of healing are asked to believe in him, and therefore in the Father who sent him. It is also the message of this book: if we want to be healed in body and spirit, we must have faith in Jesus.

ANDREW MYER is a Jesuit priest and he lectures in theology at the University of Montreal.

ISBN 085439 374 9   72 pp.

A JOURNALIST
LOOKS AT
THE LORD'S PRAYER

Italian journalist James Antonellis looks at the spiritual, social and universal implications of the Lord's Prayer with disarming honesty, clarity and charm. At every stage, the author's preoccupation as a journalist makes him search the collective conscience of his profession to see how well or badly the media acquit themselves in acting according to the sentiments of the Lord's Prayer. Here is perhaps a lesson for all the other professions too.

But underneath the author's personal and professional concern to practise what we subscribe to every time we recite the Lord's Prayer, there is the insistent vision of God, whom Jesus has taught us to call Father. Hence the boundlessness of Christian love which embraces every human being as brother or sister, free and equal, never, but never to be treated differently because of race or social status. In this spirit of charity, the author tells us, let us dare to say yet again: Our Father...

ISBN 085439 384 6   144 pp.   £4.95

A JOURNALIST LOOKS AT THE PARABLES

In these pages Italian journalist Angelo Montonati offers his personal interpretation of the parables of Jesus. They give him the cue to discuss some issues that particularly affect our society. The stories Jesus told are shown to be made-to-measure stories also for our times. With their touch of humour and irony, they penetrate the tangled mess of our contradictions and illuminate the confused hopes and fears of our century.

Thus the story of the workers in the vineyard becomes the parable of the trade unionists. The lesson of the talents is transformed into a satirical account of the error of burying ourselves in idleness. Lazarus and the rich man represent the Third World and the West being judged by God. In a society where collective blame dilutes any sense of personal sin, responsibility is the lesson to be learned from the parable of the good seed and weeds. And in the famous parable of the prodigal son the emphasis shifts from the tragedy of the son's sin to the logic of the father's prodigal love. What a moving image of God who, aching with love for humanity, 'runs wild with joy' every time one of us decides to turn over a new leaf.

ISBN 085439 385 4   144 pp.   £4.95